SHAKA THE GREAT

King of the Zulus

SHAKA THE GREAT

King of the Zulus

G. K. Osei

INPRINT EDITIONS
Baltimore

SHAKA THE GREAT

First Published 1971
Published 2001 by
INPRINT EDITIONS
All Rights Reserved.

ISBN 1-58073-030-2

Printed by BCP Digital Printing

ABOUT INPRINT EDITIONS

Our mission is to keep good books in print. We give life to books that might never be published or republished by making them available On Demand. Manuscripts and books are scanned, stored, and then printed as single or multiple copies from our digital library. When reprinting out-of-print books, we always use the best copy available.

INPRINT EDITIONS are especially useful to scholars, students, and general readers who have an interest in enjoying all that books have to offer. Our books are also a valuable resource for libraries in search of replacement copies.

Order INPRINT EDITIONS from:
Black Classic Press
P.O. Box 13414
Baltimore, MD 21203

When the Zulus march again, who will want to be a white man in South Africa?

Professor Dr. G.K. Osei

SHAKA

BIRTH OF SHAKA

Shaka the Great was born in 1786. His father was Zulu King and was called Senzangakona. He was the chief of a tribe inhabiting between the Umvolosi and Umlatusi rivers on the sea-coast. Shaka's grandfather was called Jama. His mother was Nandi. Shaka's mother is the first woman to whom Zulu history assigns greatness. The greatness of Nandi was second only to that of Shaka himself. Shaka had the heart of a lion, his military skill is above that of Caesar, he had the organizing genius of Alexander the Great, the stern discipline of Lycurgus the inflexibility of Bismarck and the destructive force of Attila. Rider Haggard said: "He was one of the most remarkable men that ever filled a throne since the days of the Pharoahs. The invincible armies of this African Attila had swept north and south east and west, and slaughtered more than a million human beings. Wherever his warriors went the blood of men, women and children was poured out without slay or stint. Indeed he reigned like a visible Death, the presiding genius of a saturnalia of slaughter."

SHAKA TAKEN AWAY

Shaka the Great was consistently being treated with contempt by the members of his town. Being by nature a man of spirit, he resented with his whole soul the attitude of his countrymen towards him. His treatment became so bad that his grandmother took him away from her daughter Nandi and went with him to her own people. Shaka's mother first fled to the Amaqwabe and then to the Mtetwa whose chief at that time was Dingiswayo.Ngomane gave Shaka a shelter in his house. Shaka never forgot this and when he became a King Shaka appointed Ngomane to be second in command of his army. It has been said that Shaka loved only his mother and Ngomane.

HE ENTERS THE SERVICE OF DINGISWAYO

Shaka the Great was taken into the service of Dingiswayo seven years after he had entered the house of Ngomane. In combats of wrestling and other matches nobody could beat

5

him. He was the best and most graceful dancer. He came first in everything he did.

Dingiswayo began his reign in 1795 when he was about twenty-five years of age. By a strong discipline he succeeded in raising himself and his people above all others along the coast. On assuming power his first act was to form his people into regiments. He had different names for the regiments and also different shields. He introduced military uniforms of a most imposing appearance to be worn by the generals and soldiers. With his new army he conquered the Quadi people. He later conquered the following people, the Qwabe, Langeni, Zulu, Ntshali, Bathelezi, Kugiwane, Thembu, Swazi and the Xhosa. The only King he had not conquered before Shaka came on the scene was Zwide, king of the Ndwande. His superior discipline insured his success. He gave orders to his generals that they were not to plunder the property of a conquered people. He requested his people to intermarry with the conquered people and so bring about a general union. Because of his kind treatment of conquered people many other states voluntarily became tributary to him and helped him in his battles. Dingiswayo opened a trade with Delagoa Bay. The trade was carried on extensively with the Portuguese. He taught his people the art of carving. Ladles of cane or wood, milk dishes, and snuff spoons were produced. A kaross manufactory was also established and a hundred men were employed in that work.

Shaka the Great enlisted in Dingiswayo's army and remained in his service until 1816. Shaka distinguished himself in battle by his courage and self-command. Before long the regiment to which he was attached became famous and Shaka himself became the favourite of Dingiswayo. Shaka the Great by his courage, industry, and perseverance raised himself from obscurity to fame. He became known as "Dingiswayo's hero". Shaka distinguished himself in battles that he was given the title of Sigidi, (thousand) in reference to the number of the enemy whom he had slained. He became Dingiswayo's favourite general because he was brave, strong, intelligent and handsome. He was liked by the soldiers because he could dance, sing, compose songs and dramatize. Shaka rose from rank to rank in Dingiswayo's army. Shaka was a born leader. His mind was vigorous as his body. He entered Dingiswayo's army unknown but he was not to remain unknown. He was hailed as the hero of Dingiswayo's army. When the Commander-in-Chief of Izicwe regiment retired the King appointed Shaka as the new commanding officer.

Shaka the Great was a man of remarkable ability and power. He studied the policy and proceedings of Dingiswayo with an attentive eye, and he soon convinced himself that he had discovered the one weak point in the new strategy. He saw clearly that Dingiswayo's generosity and forebearance was a dangerous mistake, because it left the conquered chiefs in a position to combine together at some future time against their conqueror. In his own mind he was satisfied that the only safe way to carry out such a scheme of aggression as Dingiswayo had entered upon, was to inflict such injury upon the conquered as left them no power to rise again, and he resolved that whenever he had the chance he would carry out the great system of Dingiswayo to its full and legitimate conclusion. Although Shaka had found a hiding place in the house of Dingiswayo, he never forgot where he had come from and he kept a close watch on the doings in his father's town.

DEATH OF HIS FATHER

Shaka had not to wait long for his opportunity. By the time he had served in Dingiswayo's army sufficiently long to become familiar with the system of his chief, and to make his own observations upon its defects, his father Senzangakona died, and Dingiswayo, conceiving that his brave subordinate would be a more serviceable tributary and ally than the other sons of the deceased chief, induced the Zulus to accept Shaka, at his hands, as their King.

At the time of his father's death in 1810, Shaka was only twenty-six years of age. One of his half brothers in the meantime had seized the throne. The brain-machine of Shaka was set in motion, Shaka was a genius and ranked as one of the best tacticians and strategicians the world has ever produced. As a tactician and a strategist Shaka, was beyond other leaders of his time. He decided that the one who had seized the throne had to be removed. He immediately took steps to remove the most dangerous rival Sigujana and a few others of the sons of his father. Shaka sent his half brother Ngwadi who had been with him all the time in Mtetwaland to his village Ngendeyana. Ngwadi acted as his tool. Shaka and Ngwadi concocted a tale.

He ordered his brother Ngwadi to go to his town and in

touching accents, tell how Shaka had been killed by Dingiswayo; and that Ngwadi himself narrowly escaped death at the hands of Dingiswayo and now beg for their protection. Ngwadi was well received by the people without checking his story. He became familiar with his reigning relative, gained his confidence and often accompanied him to a river to have his bath. Ngwadi was waiting for a time when the two would be alone and these visits to the river provided him with a good opportunity. On the day that Ngwadi planned to assassinate the King he concealed a couple of accomplices in the bush at the bank of the river. As the King was having his bath, two spears pierced his body from behind and nailed him there. Ngwadi and his friends ran to inform Shaka that this opponent had been removed. When Dingiswayo heard the news he sent his favourite general Shaka with an imposing staff and troops of tested soliders. Shaka said goodbye to his master, Dingiswayo. No opposition was offered to Shaka on his arrival. Any opposition would have been crushed with force. Shaka became King of the Zulus. He was the eleventh of the Zulu Kings. The Zulu Kings were Malandela 1420, Mdhalni 1460; Zulu 1500; Ntombela 1520; Nkosinkulu 1560; Mageba 1600; Punga 1640; Ndaba 1680; Jama 1720; Senzangakona 1760; Shaka 1816; Dingan 1828; Mpade 1848; and the last and one of the great Kings Cetshwayo. These kings lived and ruled successively over the Zulus. The graves of all are still pointed out there, and the place is known as Makosini, the place of Kings.

Shaka continued faithful to his old master Dingiswayo and fought in alliance with him in several campaigns. But he was altogether right in the opinion he had formed of the danger of the position. Some of the neighbouring chiefs, who had been victims of Dingiswayo's raids had at length taken a lesson out of his books, and having prepared their plans, combined against him. Dingiswayo was finally caught in advance of the main body of his army, with only a small party of followers, was taken prisoner and killed. Shaka led the combined tribes of the Mtetwas and Zulus so skilfully out of the fight, that he was forthwith accepted by both as heir common King. This was the first step made by the Zulus towards an enlargement of its influences and power.

Shaka the Great had thus a clear path opened to his ambition. He was now free to adopt his own plans of operations, and to act upon his own ideas without let or hinderance. He at once set himself to the work of establishing the Zulu supre-

8

mcy. Shaka the Great was the originator and founder of the Zulu power. Before Shaka's reign the Zulus were virtually overshadowed and esclipsed by the other people who were immediately around them; and the most considerable of these was Mtetwas. These Mtetwas dwelt in what is now the heart of Zululand, and some few miles beyond the Tugela river.

BECOMES KING OF THE ZULUS

Shaka knew that on this planet the wise man and the strong man, the man who is respected is the man who knows how to use his sword. He was a man of fixed principle and it was not his habit to abandon anything, until he had brought it to an end according to his wishes. He mounted the Zulu throne at the age of twenty-six and at once set forth to unite the people under one strong King. His ambition was to establish a strong black empire with one King. He looked to the East, West, North and South and all the people were living in peace and he said: "I shall rule over them all. There shall be one chief instead of many and that chief, myself." Shaka made only one mistake in his life and that was immediately he came to power. Inexperience in all the rules of statecraft and the perils of sovereignty, he permitted the most dangerous rivals, to continue their intrigues alongside him; which fraternal trust eventually cost him his life.

When Shaka mounted the throne Isanusi advised him to choose a name for his country. Shaka said to Isanusi: "You are right Isanusi. Today I shall find myself a tribe-name that is well sounding, such as none other has ever had." Isanusi asked: "What name?" Shaka said: "Zulu, Amazulu" (Heaven and People of Heaven). Isanusi asked: "Why do you choose this name?" "Amazulu". As soon as Isanusi had finished his question there was a thunder. Shaka said "Because I am great, I am as this cloud that has thundered. I, too, look upon the tribes and they are in fear."

GOVERNMENT

The Zulus were unimportant before the time of their celebrated Shaka the Great. Under Shaka's leadership a new era commenced for his people. He converted a nation of pedlars of tobacco into a nation of warriors. Whether Shaka was cruel or wicked no one can deny the fact that he was a great man. Shaka appears in the early history of Natal as a great man. He extended his empire eight hundred miles north, south, and west. The Zulus became a dreaded power in the hands of Shaka. During Shaka's reign the Zulus were able to grow their crops and their cattle, and move about in safety. He conquered in rapid succession all the other countries around Zululand. Europe did not know anything about Zululand until Shaka made it famous. The Zulu government was established by Shaka. In his reign there was no tomorrow for the Zulus, who therefore replied to every promise with the proverb, Give it today; before tomorrow I may be killed. The government was hereditary and theorethically absolute but in practice the King was not so, being "obliged to consider what effect his commands will have on the minds of his followers. Even Shaka, one of the greatest despots who ever governed any nation, constantly kept this consideration in view, being perfectly aware that his reign would soon terminate, if he opposed the general will of his people."

On certain matters Shaka did not act without consulting with his chief officers, and being assured he should carry the nation with him. He mounted the Zulu throne by a course of very carefully prepared plans, and by such tact and policy in their execution; and, only when he felt himself secure, did he rear his majestic head. The prime ministers of Zululand during Shaka's reign were Sotole and Bosombosa. The two "great nobles", who, with him formed a sort of triumvirate government, were called "the two eyes, ears, or arms of the monarch". The existence of a council, in which all matters of importance were discussed at length, was a check upon the power of the King. Shaka had all the machinery for reaching the remote and insignificant people in his realm. It is interesting to show in brief outline crimes and their punishments during the reign of Shaka. Treason, as contriving the death of a chief; conveying information to the enemy was punished by death and confiscation. Murder was punished by death or fine according to the circumstances. Poisoning and practices with an evil intent was punished by death and confiscation. Rape, punished by fine and sometimes by death.

Adultery — fine; sometimes death; maiming — fine; false witness — heavy fine; theft — restitution and fine; causing cattle to abort — heavy fine and injuring cattle — death or fine according to circumstances. There were three different courts to which the accused was brought according to the relative magnitude of the crime. The heads of the villages decided all the minor offences that were committed; graver crimes were tried by tribunals connected with the principal ministers; and the King with the assistance of his ministers tried all the gravest crimes.

Shaka the Great improved agriculture and cattle rearing was given a special attention. The Zulu sets a high value on his cattle. To his mind they represent several ideas. Cattle enabled him to marry; cows were needed to rear a family; oxen furnished sacrifices wherewith to propitate the spirits. The Zulu esteemed his cattle very highly. Before Shaka's time, cattle-stealing, was very prevalent among his people. He forbade cattle-stealing, among his people and punished it with death. Shaka improved agriculture and many grass-woven grass bags were made throughout Zululand. The purpose for making the bags was only known to Shaka. He made property more secure. No man was allowed to marry till Shaka gave his consent. The young soldiers were forbidden to take wives, that they might not be enervated by domestic influences, and distracted from their military duties by domestic habits and ties. Shaka institut-ed an invariable law, that any young soldier who returned from a fight without shield or spear, or with disgraceful stamp of a wound upon his back, should pay the forfeit of his life. Shaka not only employed his warriors against the beasts of the field, but frequently against the birds. New towns were also built by Shaka. Courts were established and justice ad-ministered to all without favours. Before Shaka's reign there was an institution called the Feast of First Fruits. This was an act of thanksgiving for the fruits of the earth. Shaka added to this feast certain military rites, and gave it much more the aspect of a war-feast. During this festival soldiers who had served very well and were old were discharged from military duties and were allowed to marry. New songs were composed for this occassion. Shaka was not a selfish man. He was also fair in the administration of justice. Shaka did not interfere with the liberty of individuals as long as his laws were obeyed.

All his laws were enacted with the view of building one great Black Empire. Shaka possessed a most surprising influence over his people. They were ready, at his command, to undertake the most perilous work; and a man has been known even to thank him while the executioners were beating him to death. Here is what a man Shaka had condemned to death said before he was beheaded: "Tell them (his children) and hearken to all ye young warriors, that the Zulus now have a chief of chiefs — age, greater even than Zulu himself, from whose loins we all sprang, and whose name we now all bear. Tell them I was blind not to have seen this long ago, and that I deserve my fate for getting in the path of the Great Elephant, who is now stamping me flat, but has spared my kraal. Tell them I die gladly now, for our Great Elephant will stamp out our lifelong enemies, the Butelezi, who have so often inflicted grievous humiliations on us, and he will eat up all the surrounding tribes, and make the Zulus great. Finally, tell them that it is my wish, and my command, that they fight for the new chief till they die."

HOW HE MAINTAINED HIMSELF IN POWER

How did Shaka the Great maintain his influence over his people? Shaka always had good advisers and efficient administrators around him. Two of these people were Mgobozi whom Shaka offered the post of Commander-in-Chief but he refused because he was an old man; and Pampata a girl of twenty-four years old. She acquainted Shaka with all the rumours, trends of opinion, approval or criticism of his policy and what the people were planning to do. Shaka was general enough to know that the intelligence department is the first line of a nation's defence. The head of his spy network was called Nollebe. Shaka always gave personal attention to the needs of the soldiers and he was very liberal in his gifts. He also told his soldiers that they could all gain promotion on their merits. He said that as soon as a man from any clan joined the Zulu army the person became a Zulu. Shaka promoted Nzobo of the Ntombela's to be the commander of the Izim-Pohlo and his famous field marshal Mdlaka of the Gazini to command the Fasimba regiment. It was his policy that any man who served him well could rise to great position and wealth. Shaka at no time broke the custom of the Zulus. When Mgobozi wanted to marry and had to pay the necessary number of cattle needed for a bride Shaka himself paid it for him. Shaka could have selected a wife for him without paying the dowry but he did according to custom.

When Shaka's granfather died Shaka was in the town where the old man lived. A day after Mbiya his granfather had died, he made all the funeral arrangements and left the same day without attending the funeral. According to the Zulu custom if he had stayed for the funeral he would have had to remain for a month after the burial to observe all the necessary ceremonies. At the great Zulu Harvest Festival Shaka by custom had to drink certain medicine prepared for him. He observed this custom and told Pampata that the beneficial effect of the medicine was psychological and had nothing to do with their constitution.

According to custom Shaka had to delay his appearance, when the soldiers singing approached his hut at the Harvest Festival and shouted for him to coming out. Shaka had to wait until the Royal women joined in the song before coming out. As it has been stated above Shaka saw to it that the soldiers were well fed. He was liberal in distributing the spoils of war among his soldiers. The best spoils always went to the ordinary soldiers. Shaka's civilians were diverted by amusements. These means, however, would have been very inefficious, if used alone: he employed two others, which operated with greater force, namely Justice and Severity. The severity with which he acted, contributed to establish Shaka's power. Death was inflicted for all important crimes. To prevent intercession he never gave his reason for ordering an execution until it was too late to recall the sentence. Shaka always insisted on inspecting everything himself. He always checked all reports brought to him by his agents by collateral evidence. After having established a strong force of over six hundred thousand men, about a hundred thousand of which were warriors in constant readiness for battle, and forming his whole force into regiments, he began to elect rulers, to abolish the old laws, and enact new ones.

CREATION OF AN ARMY

When Shaka finished consolidating his position at home he turned his attention to pressing needs of the state. The pressing need was to have adequate defence and offensive forces. There was no Zulu army so he set out to create one. Shaka coined all the Zulu regimental names at the time he reorganized the Zulu army. The names of the regiments were obvious, being taken generally from some incident in the history of the Zulus or peculiarity in their behaviour. Thus one was called the Panther-Catcher, by reason of a leopard which Shaka once commanded them to catch and kill. Another regiment was called the Bees, in allusion to their numerical strength, imitating in battle the buzzing of bees as well as the stinging propensities of those insects. The men between 30-40 years of age he put them together and called them AmaWombe.

He built for these soldiers a new barracks and called it UmBelebele (the Everlasting Pest). For the men born between 1785-90 he put them together and called them UDubintalangu, alias in Tontela. He put them in his father's barracks called Isiklebe. Those born between 1790-95 he called them UmGamule or UDlambedlu. This group formed the Bachelors' Brigade. It must be remembered that only the first army was allowed to marry. Shaka gathered together all the idle boys of about (twenty years of age and formed them into a new regiment. He called this army Fasimba (the Haze). This army was stationed at Bulawayo his new Capital. So gladly did they respond to his effective training that they became henceforth his favourite regiment "Shaka's Own". The soldiers were not allowed to marry. Shaka said that when men were being killed in battle, the married man thought of his wife and children, so that he ran away. He said that the unmarried soldier fought to kill and to conquer, so that he might enjoy the praises of the young ladies.

Shaka the Great subjected the army under his command to more rigid discipline than had been previously enforced. He created an army which was kept always ready, at an hour's notice, to march fifty miles in any direction without a half and "eat up" a town. Shaka created the most powerful military power that has ever existed on the African continent. With a new army at his command Shaka now embarked upon his career of uniting all the Black people. Shaka consolidated his position at home before he embarked upon his career of conquest. The economy was strong and freedom and justice was administered to all. Shaka reorganized the people for political solidarity to support military conquest. Roads were built to facilitate contact with the Capital. The capital was called Umgungundhlovu (The Elephant Abode). In the midst of the city was a large courtyard for drilling his regiments. On this spot assembled the troops from war as victors bringing the cattle and other property to present as spoils to the King. Feasts and state functions took place here. Near this Central courtyard lived the advisers as lieutenants of the chief. The best cattle were kraaled there, and near the enclosure stood the court of the chief. It had two entrances guarded by warriors. Everyone entering shouted his greeting, leaving his spear and blanket at the door with the guards. He must prostrate himself, crawl forward on his stomach and say "Bayete", and he remained in this position until his greeting was received.

At the second entrance of the Court was a high rock which the watchman sat day and night. No one was allowed to enter the city by night. From the court was a palisade leading to the 'chief's hut, Ndhlunkulu (the great house) to which one came under penalty of death unless called by a messenger of the chief. In other part live the city guards. The whole Zulu nation was organized into a great military camp. They owed their military power to Shaka the Great. The Zulus under Shaka the Great first tasted the joy of military prestige and the pride of victorious arms. Shaka, the founder of Zulu military system, is the man round whose name the glorious tradition of Zulu conquest cling. Some of Shaka's most important towns were Isikelpe, Gibinegu, Dukusa, Nobamba, Bulawayo, Umbelebele, and Utukusu. Utukusu was built on the Umvoti after he had subdued this district. Here he passed much of his time during the latter part of his life, praised and worshipped, by his soldiers and all the people, as "the tiger, the lion, the elephant, the great mountain, the mighty black prince, king of kings, the immortal only one." Two of the songs which his soldiers used to sing in his praise, turned into English run thus:

Thou striker of poison into every conspirator,
As well those abroad as those who'er at home;
Thou art green as the gull of the groat;
Butterfly of Punga, tinted with circling spots,
As if made the twilight from the shadows of mountains,
In the dusk of the evening, when the wizards are abroad;
Lynx-eyed descendant of Punga and Makeba,
With looking at whom I am ever entranced.
What beautiful parts! a calf of the cow!
The kicking of this cow confuses my brain,
Kicking the milker and accepting the holder.

Thou didst finish, finish the nations;
Where will you go to battle now?
Hey! where will you go to battle now?
Thou didst conquer the kings,
Where do you go to battle now:
Thou didst finish, finish the nations,
Where do you go to battle now?
Hurrah! hurrah! hurrah!
Where do you go to battle now?

The sound of a war-song at the Zulu-court, where thousands of voices were combined, has been described as overpowering. Every festival and every grand ceremony or rejoicing was celebrated by a review and display of regiments. Reviews took place at the great place of the King, where songs, dances, and chivalrous games were all made use of to increase the military enthusiasm of the soldiers. At the annual harvest festival the army was allowed more freedom of speech. The soldiers could question Shaka and was bound to reply to all the questions asked. On these occasions, the soldiers were called upon to go through their exercise and manoeuvres, and to show their proficiency in martial movements before the assembled chiefs and courtiers, whose plaudits stimulate them sometimes to a perfect pitch of frenzy. Shaka the great was the founder of the national feeling among the Zulus.

Shaka the Great saw, thought and learned much in Dingiswayo's military school. Some of the methods did not please him. The method of throwing an assagai at a distant enemy was to him as though merely throwing one's weapon away. He warned his soldiers that these weapons should not be thrown at the enemy. Shaka abolished the long throwing assagai. Before he directed his soldiers to depart from the usage of their forefathers, he ordered a mock fight between two regiments, reeds being substituted for more dangerous arms. The one regiment was told to follow the old-fashioned practice, and cast their reeds at the enemy; the other, each man having a single reed, was to rush upon the opposing rank and use their fragile weapons at close quarters. After a certain time Shaka sent his generals to count how many bodymarks as representative of wounds each man had received; and when it was reported to him the men armed with the stabbing assagai had only one or two marks each, but that the others were covered with marks, Shaka ordained that the invariable arms of the Zulu warrior in future should always be the stabbing assagai in one hand and a shield in another. All soldiers were to return from battle with their weapons, or not return at all. The substitution of the short assagai, compelled the Zulus to fight hand-to-hand.

The method of fighting an enemy merely to exercise a momentary power over him did not satisfy him. Shaka was interested in wiping out his enemies. He once said: "Strike an enemy once and for all let him cease to exist as a tribe or he will live to fly at your throat again." If an enemy were worth conquering at all, he was worth crushing out of existence once and for all. Whatever was to be feared in the enemy must be removed forever. Whatever was good and serviceable must be taken by the victorious nation as a reward of its victory and use to consolidate its own position. Shaka was liberal in his gifts to those who had been so fortunate as to earn his favour; and he was ruthless to all his opponents.

ABOLITION OF SHOES IN HIS ARMY

Shaka abolished the use of shoes since they prevented his soldiers from running very fast. When he abolished the use of sandals there was consternation among the older soldiers as well as some of the young ones. A month after he had abolished the use of sandals Shaka noticed that there was still some soldiers who were not willing and mumuring against his order. Shaka at once ordered the Fasimba regiment to collect many basketsful of the three-pronged 'devil thorns' which was avoided by all those, travelling without shoes. When the regiment reported that it had collected enough, Shaka ordered them to be strewn over the parade ground at Bulawayo. Orders were issued for all the regiments to parade a little away from the ground covered with the thorns. Shaka then addressed the soldiers: "My children it has come to my ears that some of you have dainty feet and this has surely grieved my heart. In my fatherly kindness I have decided to help you to harden your feet so that you will never have occassion again to complain about them. The parade ground has therefore been strewn with the three-pronged 'devils thorns' which you will proceed to stamp out of sight with your bare feet. Now, my children, it is my will that you should do this with gusto, to prove how gladly you obey my commands. Those who hesitate, or who stamp gingerly, will be disobedient to my commands, and disobedience merits death. My slayers are at hand. Now go to it with a will."

The soldiers gritted their teeth and singing their war song, spread over the parade ground. Shaka himself was the first person to parade the ground. His feet, however, from long exposure, were hard, horny and impervious. Shaka turned and faced the soldiers and as he led in stamping his eyes picked out those who were not willing to stamp. These soldiers he approached with his slayers and clubbed to death. After a dozen had been killed the rest of the soldiers stamped with a frenzy in which they tried to outdo each other. After sometime Shaka dismissed the soldiers by saying: "I thank you, my children for your zeal in carrying out my will, which you will soon learn is the only law in your lives and in the land I rule. Now take these oxen and eat heartily, and let there be generous measures of beer, which you will find awaiting you. For you have done your duty and deserve reward." After this parade the soldiers never complained again.

NEW ATTACK FORMATION.

Shaka also changed the attack formation, modelling it after the shape of a bull's horns. In the centre were the main body and the reinforcements, while two forward flanks curved out to enclose the enemy.

Shaka kept spies all over the country. He kept up a system of espionage, by which he knew at all times the condition and strength of every tribe around him, both independent and tributary; and these persons were always directed to make such observations on the passes to and from the country to which they were sent, as might be useful in leading the troops to the scene of action with the surest chance of arriving at their position, without being discovered on the one hand, or surprised on the other. Shaka was general enough to know that the intelligence department is the first line of a nation's defence. The head of this spy net work was called Nollebe. Shaka kept his plans to himself and only informed the generals selected for a special piece of service what the plan was. Every kind of treachery and deceit was practiced by him. Shaka will wait until his enemy could be taken at a favourable time. He discovered that the surest and simplest method of conquering people was to take them by suprise. Shaka trusted nobody. Nandi, his mother, was the only person in the world he was prepared to trust. Shaka never allowed Europeans to trade with his subjects. All selling and buying had to be done with him. He also did not allow Europeans who visited him to travel freely in his country. Their movements were restricted.

COMPOSITION OF THE ARMY

From a mere five hundred undisciplined soldiers he increased the number to six hundred thousand soldiers whose discipline exceeded that of the Spartans, the Roman legions, and the Prussians at their best. Shaka taught them obedience. When the soldiers received an order they were not to answer back or ask the reason why, but simply do what they were ordered. The army was divided into many divisions and each division had a fieldmarshal at the top and had its own colours. Five of his best fieldmarshals were Mziligazi, Manukuza, Qnetu, Mgobozi, and Mdlaka a famous field marshal. If a division disgraced itself he ordered no inquiry but sent another division to wipe it out. "There has probably never been," says one writer, "a more perfect system of discipline than that by which chief Tshaka ruled his army and kingdom. At a review an order might be given in the most unexpected manner which meant death to hundreds. If the regiment hesitated or dared to remonstrate, so perfect was the discipline and so great the jealousy that another was ready to cut them down. A warrior returning home from battle without his arms was put to death without trial. A general returning unsuccessful in the main purpose of his expedition shared the same fate."

The Zulu army composed of the entire nation capable of bearing arms. The following method was employed in recuriting the soldiers. At short intervals, differing from two to five years, all the young men who had during that time attained the age of fourteen were formed into a regiment and after a year's probation was placed at a military kraal. When the young regiment was numerous, they built a new military kraal. As the regiment grew old, it generally had one or more regiments embodied with it, so that the young men had the benefit of their elder's experience and when the latter died out the young ones took their place and kept up the name and prestige of their military kraal.

THE REGIMENTS

A Zulu regiment consisted of about 1,000 soldiers. They were men of the same age and between the regiments there was a spirit of great rivalry and competition. Each regiment had its own songs besides the national war-songs. When the regiments were marching to war each sang its own songs, but during the actual fighting, the national song was always used. The regiments wore different uniforms and had shields painted with regimental colours. No two regiments had the same kind of shields.

Some regiments had white and black shield, white shield with black spots. Far more impressive was the regimental dress

19

of the soldiers which in many instances was extremely rich and beautiful. The head-dress of the Isangu regiment consisted of "a grotesque fillet of white ox-hide with lappets of the same of a red colour. On the back of the head was a shaved ball of eagle or bustard feathers, and two bunches of the long tail of the Kaffir-finch formed graceful ornaments as they floated in the air."

The warriors were armed with a shield, one or two throwing assagai, and one stabbing one. In Shaka's days they were armed only with one stabbing assagai an a shield. The shields were made from the hides of Shaka's cattle. The married soldiers were regarded as "inferior" and they carried red shields. Distinguished soldiers had white shields with one or two black spots. The shields of the young ones were black. Shaka's military dress consisted of monkey's skins, in three folds from his waist to the knee, from which two white cows' tails were suspended, as well as from each arm; round his head was a neat band of fur stuffed, in front of which was placed a tall feather, and on each side a variegated plume. The respective regiments were also distinguished by the shape and ornament of their caps. Soldiers who distinguished themselves in war were decorated. Beads and other ornaments were given to such men. There was a necklace consisted of a number of pieces of a certain kind of root strung on sinew, or bits of wood, each one representing an enemy slain. To those who had been outstanding brave in battle the King gave presents of cattle.

MILITARY CAMPS

Each regiment had its own military camp. During Shaka's reign the military camps were spread out over the country, and kept apart from the rest of the people, and even from their wives and children. The situations of military camps were selected with the greatest care. The camps were placed under the most approved and loyal leaders. Some of Shaka's best fieldmarshals and generals were Mdlaka, son of Nadi of the Gazini clan, Mzilikazi of the Kumalos, Mgobozi whom Shaka offered the post of Commander-in-Chief but he refused, Ngomane who rose to be second in command of the army, and a prime minister, Ngoboka of the Sokulus, Ndleba who became a prime minister, Nzobo of the Ntombelas and commander of the Izim-Pohlo, and Nkomendala. These commanders helped

Shaka to build the Zulu nation. Shaka the Great, Sunni Ali, Mdlaka, Mgobozi, Mzilikazi, Osei Tutu, Askia the Great and Mosheshes' brilliancy as soldiers and statesmen outshone that of Cromwell, Napoleon, Caesar, Alexander of Macedonia, Wellington and Washington: hence they are entitled to the highest place as heroes among men. Africa has produced countless numbers of men and women in war and in peace, whose lustre and bravery outshines that of any other people.

The huts were built on a circle form and were divided up into sections, the most important was the Isigodlo which occupied the top end. At the head of each ikhanda was an induna. The induna had great power and saw to it that all the men in his military district rendered a reasonable amount of service each year at the ikhanda. Every induna of military camp had the right in occurrances of a sudden and local kind, such as a raid or insurrection, to call out the men under his command. Shaka the Great gave the indunas power to impose the death penalty. Dingan restricted this power to three of his chief indunas only, viz Dambuza, Wohlo and uMdlela. The Indunas were permitted to live with their wives, but for the rest, with the exception of the Isigodlo, no women were permitted to live in an ikhanda, and children were rigidly proscribed. Below the induna were an officer second in command and two wing officers; then came captains of the amaviyo. Below the Captains were two or three junior officers.

Each of the regiments had the same internal formation. They were in the first place divided equally into two wings — the right wing and the left — and in the second were subdivided into companies from ten to two hundred soldiers. The soldiers were fed on beer, meat and other food stuffs. Grain grown in the King's farms were used in making the beer. Shaka supplied the whole food of the soldiers. When the soldiers were not fighting Shaka used them to repair or construct camps, fences, cattle enclosures; or they hoed, sowed, weeded and harvested the crops. Soldiers were used to carry grains to other parts of the country and some also carried messages to officers in all parts of the country. Bryant has described the life at the barracks in his book. He says: "while ease and freedom were abundant, stern discipline continuously reigned, but it was wholly a moral force, the young men being thrown entirely on their honour, without standing regulations and without supervision (this is not correct there were laws to regulate their conduct)... They were there for the sole purpose of fulfilling the king's behests. They acted as the state army, the state police, the state labour gang. They fought the clan's battles, made raids when state funds were low. They slew convicted and even suspected malefactors and confiscated their property in the king's name; they built and repaired the king's kraal, cultivated his fields and manufactured his war-shields. . . It was their duty to the state as men, and they did it without question or complaint." There were many regulations which the soldiers had to obey and they were also surpervised by the commanding officers who had power to impose the death penalty. As it has already been pointed out soldiers were not permitted to marry. No one in Zululand, male or female was permitted to marry without the direct permission of Shaka the Great. He would release a certain regiment of old men to marry and would also release a regiment of girls from which the men would choose their wives. When asked why soldiers were not allowed to marry Shaka replied, "Marriage for young warriors is folly. Their first and last duty is to protect the nation from its enemies. This they cannot do effectively if they have family ties. When they reached a mature age, and have also proved their worth, I am prepared to consider individual cases, and even whole regiments, if they have shown except-ional merit. But, until the nation has been made secure against all external enemies, the marriage ban will be strictly enforced on all warriors, saving only in quite exceptional cases." Shaka went on to tell the soldiers, "Look at Mgobozi. One such man will produce better fighting stock than twenty untried young warriors who are allowed to marry indiscriminately. Do we not now select the bulls of our heards? Should we then be less careful in selecting the right fathers for the future children of Zululand? I tell you all, in future a man will have to prove his worth to be a father, before he receives permission to marry. I will not tolerate the propagation of our race by untried men, who may be undesirable fathers. Finally, look at me, all you who are my age-mates and below. Although I am the King and have all power, I have not taken a wife. I have told you the true reason but, apart from that, there is too much fighting ahead to allow me to dally with women, and you all know that I have not touched a single one of the um-dlunkulu women. None of you can therefore complain that I ask you to stop where I do not stop, any more than I did when I led you on to the field of thorns, and showed you how to stamp them down before I asked you to do so."

After Shaka had finished speaking the soldiers applauded and shouted, "He is indeed a chief of chiefs, for he never asks us to do anything, which he himself does not do first. Who is there who is like him? lead us, father, and we will follow until we eat earth. Say but the word, son of Heaven, and it shall be done. Bayete!"

Boys joined the army at the age of thirteen. At seventeen after rigorous disciplining and training, they were assigned to a regiment. Day after day the children never met their parents. The children were well trained. Their talk, their song, their games... all were of war. Everything they heard, saw, or did was connected with war. The Fasimba was the most fearsome of Zulu regiments. None of these youths was allowed to speak to a girl. Their business, Shaka told them, was war not love. Everything was to be carried out in conformity with military needs. Shaka put an end to circumcision in his country because the time required for this rite could be spent in preparation for war. Warriors who had learned to fight were distinguished from those in training. Only soldiers who had distiguished themselves in war were allowed to select their wives later. Divorce was not permitted. The interest of the nation came first, Shaka preached. He saw to it that the soldiers were well fed. Determined, ambitious, far-seeing, Shaka soon changed the face of the surrounding country. His system of training and discipline was admirable for the object he had in view. His army being formed, drilled, and disciplined, Shaka soon began to test its prowess. In his army Shaka insisted on quality rather than quantity. He was a man who was not prepared to take chances.

THE TIME THE ZULUS WENT TO WAR

The Zulus always went to war in the winter months after the crops had been harvested. In the summer-time dancing was resorted to, and new songs were composed, as it was considered disgraceful to sing the songs of the previous years. On these occassions the regiments sang before the King, particularly at the harvest season, when those who excel received the applause of the King, and not infrequently got cattle, which afforded the soldiers a subject for conversation and amusement, until the harvest was all gleaned. Before war was declared, the King always summoned his counsellors, most of them were generals of the various regiments. To get the generals to approve of the declaration of war was very essential. Issacs who visited Shaka says that he was always at variance with half of his commanders, and prevented their meeting by having their regiments some distant apart. To mobilise the soldiers Shaka sent and order to the camp commanders, ordering all soldiers to come to the Great Palace. Within twenty-four hours those regiments which were stationed within fifteen miles of the Great Palace had already assembled at the place they were ordered to be, and within a time of two to five days the whole army was at the Palace. The regiments camped apart.

In spite of the shortest time the soldiers were required to mobilise, no soldier went to war unless he first visited his home to pray to his ancestral spirits for protection. No expedition took place without an offering and prayers to the ancestors. When soldiers were summonded to war, it was customary for them to put on their battledress and enter the cattle kraal with great solemnity. Before marching, a circle or umkumbi was formed inside the kraal each company together, their officers in an inner ring — the first and second command in the centre. The regiment then proceeds to break into companies, beginning from the left hand side, each company forming a circle, and marching off, followed by boys carrying provisions. The company officers marched immediately in rear of their men, the second in command in the rear left wing and the Commanding Officer in the rear of the right. Before marching off, the regiments reform companies under their respective officers, and the regiment selected by the King to take the lead advances. The march was in order of companies for the first day, after which it was continued in the umsila. The baggage and provision bearers fell in rear of the column on the second day; and the cattle composing the commissariat were driven between them and the rear most regiment, until near the enemy. The order of companies was then resumed, and on coming in sight, the whole army again formed an umkumbi, for the purpose of enabling the C-in-C to address the men, and give his final instructions, which concluded, the different regiments intended to commence the attack did so. A single body of troops, as a reserve, remained seated with their backs to the enemy.

LAST ADDRESS BEFORE BATTLE

Before the soldiers went to war it was customary for the King to address them. Shaka imposed hard rules upon himself and lived up to them. Shaka's whole being was concentrated on supremacy. Once he had disciplined himself he imposed his discipline on others. His motto in war was literally "Death or Victory." One day on the eve of a battle Shaka addressed his soldiers like this: My Companions, I am much troubled. I cannot sleep or have any peace of heart. I have already told you that those you are going to meet are men and not children. And I repeat you must know that you will be facing death. Whoever is afraid, let him return at once. I do not demand that you fight. But all who stay must understand that they may not turn back, whatever happens. They must die with their chief, or conquer with him." The soldiers said "Where we are commanded to go, we will go, even if it be to death." There was but one way for a Zulu Soldier to march, Shaka told his men and that was forward. Should the Zulu regiment return unsuccessful from the fray, no matter whether it had fought bravely or otherwise the punishment for defeat was death. By Shaka's law, it was death or victory. Thus, the Zulu may be said to fight with a rope round his neck. He dares not fail least failure should bring more punishment — death with dishonour. If a man was observed to show the slightest hesitation about coming to close quarters with the enemy, he was executed as soon as the fight was over. Shaka's Soldiers never ran away in a battle. If the soldiers would not die rather than fly, they must die for flying. To conquer or die was their motto, and engraven upon their mighty shields. Forced either to conquer or die, the soldiers of Shaka constituted the greatest fighting force ever developed in Africa. Cowards were slaughtered by the thousands. Before this military machine thrones and seats of governments tumbled. With such a system of carefully planned organisation, wielded by a large measure of ability, and sustained by a ruthless purpose and will, it is by no means surprising that the name of Shaka soon became a terror and a power. By 1820 Shaka had made South Africa ring with his name. After conquring the people around, he bore his victorious arms further, and carried fire and sword along the slopes of the Drakensberg. In the year 1824, Shaka was about in the zenith of his power, and Zulus had become a formidable people. Chiefs and their vassals trembled when they heard of the approach of Shaka's army.

All neighbouring tribes came under his sway or underwent desolation and extermination at the hands of Shaka's soldiers.

CONCEALMENT OF DESTINATION

The destination of the soldiers was concealed till the time of starting and then was revealed to one general. Shaka in his speech to the soldiers often hinted at a different destination from the actual one. Isaacs says "When all was ready for entering upon their march, he confined to one general his design, and to him he entrusted the command, should he not head his army in person. He, however, never confined in one man but on one occasion; upon no occasion whatever did he repeat such confidence. He made it an invariable rule always to address his warriors at their departure, and his language was generally studied to raise their expectations, and excited them in the hour of battle. He particularly detailed to them the road his spies had pointed out, inducing them to believe that they were going to attack any party but the one actually designed, and known only to the general-in-chief. This was judicious, because it kept his real object from being known, and, at the same time, prevented any trencherous communikation to his enemy, who might get early intimation of his intended attack." He was exceedingly wary, and used great precaution in concealing even from his generals or chiefs, the power or tribe with whom he designed combating; nor until the eve of marching did he make known to them the object of their expedition. By this he evinced some discretion, and precluded the possibility of his enemy being apprised of his intentions.

The soldiers marched in extended columns. The scouts were in front, on the flanks and the rear. When the soldiers were far from the place where they were to engaged the enemy they often rolled up their shields and carried them on their backs. Carriers were assigned to every regiment to carry the belongings of the generals. The Zulu Army had no commissariat and transport. The former consisted of three or four days' provision, in the form of millet or Maize, and a heard of cattle, proportioned to the distance to be covered, accompanied each regiment. The latter consisted of a number of boys who followed each regiment, carrying the sleeping mats, blankets, and provisions, and assisted to drive the cattle.

The Zulus could march fifty miles a day and at the end give a battle. Whenever the soldiers came to a river in flood which was out of their depth but did not extend over fifteen yards in breadth, the soldiers plunged into it in a dense mass, holding on to one another, those behind pushing those in front forward, and in this way they succeeded in crossing the stream.

Countersigns and passwords were used by the soldiers when they were travelling at night. When the soldiers reached the enemy territory, they marched in closer formation and divided into two. An advance guard of ten companies went ten to twelve miles ahead to decieve the enemy that they were the main body and it was held to be a serious breach in tactics for the soldiers to fail to act like this. Spies were sent out to locate the enemy, and as soon as the advance guard found it had been seen by the enemy, scouts were sent to warn the main body. Spies were also sent out before an expedition. Thus, when Shaka had determined to attack the Amampondo, persons were despatched to examine the country, find out the enemy's strong-holds, and ascertain how these might be approached from some point whence an attack would be best expected. When fighting was about to take place, the soldiers were drawn up in semicircle and orders were given by the supreme commander as to the routes to be taken, what regiments were to form the left and the right horns. The Zulus attacked in the form of a semicircle, usually making a feint with one horn, while the other swept round to surround the enemy. The center consisted of the greatest number of soldiers, and also the best soldiers advanced to crush the enemy. Behind the center was a large force which came to their aid whenever the need arose. Their skirmishing was, extremely good, and was performed even under a heavy fire with the utmost order and regularity. Their officers had their regulated duties and responsibilities, according to their rank, and the men lent a ready obedience to their orders. The army was accompanied by doctors, who carried bundles of medicine with which to treat the soldiers. The army doctors not only prepared the soldiers for war, but also treated the wounded. When Isaac was wounded during the expedition against Phakathwayo, in which he accompanied Shaka's Army, he was treated by the doctors.

AFTER AN EXPEDITION

After an expedition the soldiers were allowed to return to their villages for a short period. Stuart says that after an expedition the soldiers first went to the King and there gave an account of the war before returning to their homes. The troops on returning from a war sang their war song and as soon as the women heard them they came with faces smeared with light-coloured clay, shrieking "Ki Ki Ki... Kuhle Kwethu" (Joy in our homes), at the top of their voices as a welcome.

A hero received as many as ten heard of cattle from the King. In Shaka's days cowards received the death penalty. There is still pointed out in Zululand, near Undini, a round bush, called by the Zulus, "The Coward's Bush". Here it was that Shaka used to review his soldiers on their return from an expedition. Here it was he meted out praise and blame to his captains and their men. In the days of Mpade and Cetshwayo cowards were not killed but suffered many indignities. At the return of Shaka's soldiers from an expedition, he was always generous to them, it must be admitted, but that only occurred in the case of their having achieved a victory over his enemies; in such cases he gave the captured spoils liberally amongst them.

Shaka was a man of strong principles. He feared nobody obeyed nobody, and considered nobody. Everything must be sacrificed to the end of creating a Black Empire. Neither sentiment, nor love, nor religion must interfere with his reaching the goal of establishing a great Black Empire. Shaka was the first person in the world to advocate a continental union of all Black People. His aim was to create an Empire of Black People governed by Black People for the Black People. A man must have some positive convictions, some clear-cut and well-defined ideas and policies to make an impression upon the world. Pursing his policy of creating a Black Empire, he conquered one tribe after another, located them here and there among his own people, taking care so to distribute, guard and govern them, as to hold them in the most complete awe and subordination to himself. In this way he increased the number of his people and tributaries, the strength of his army, and the extent of his diminions. In 1822 his power was felt at least half the continent of Africa. His quick movement from place to place as he went conquering is aptly portrayed in Umlilo wothathe ubuhanguhangu (The wild fire of dried grass consuming fiercely).

WAR WITH ZWIDE

At the time that Dingiswayo was very busy building his army there was another King who was very powerful. He was called Zwide. Dingiswayo was married to Zwide's sister but because of the killing of Malusi, Zwide's half brother, by Zwide, the relationship between Zwide and Dingiswayo became strained. War was waged and Dingiswayo was killed. He was captured by Zwide's men and Zwide's mother Ntombazi persuaded him to kill Dingiswayo. Fynn says that Shaka betrayed Dingiswayo to Zwide. He writes: "The experience he had gained during his attendance on Dingiswayo and his own ambitious views, could not find scope for action so long as his protector was alive. Chaka took the earliest opportunity of ridding himself of such an obstacle. Dingiswayo having gone to attack the chief Zwide, Chaka accompanied him, commanding one division of the force, and knowing the spot where Dingiswayo would post himself to observe the battle secretly communicated this knowledge to the enemy who sent a force and took him prisoner". This, however, is not correct. When Dingiswayo started on the campaign against Zwide Shaka had gone to take his father's throne. Dingiswayo sent a message to Shaka to meet him at the appointed place on a certain day. Shaka did not arrive on time and when arrived Dingiswayo had been killed. Writing of this same incident Bryant says: "It was a very short while, therefore, before Zwide had heard all about Donda's intrigue — how he had kept the enemy, Shaka, au courant with events proceeding in Ndwandweland, and so led him to return home instead of walking, like Dingiswayo, straight into Zwide's lair."

Zwide's act of killing Dingiswayo made Shaka furious and he decided to avenge the blood of his benefactor. It was necessary for him to defeat Zwide. Shaka had made up his mind that Zululand was not big enough for many Kings, and that it was desirable that all tribes pay homage to him. As it has already been said the Zulus were not powerful until Shaka came on the scene. Shaka's father had been paying homage to Zwide and had promised to send to Zwide three maidens as a sign of his friendship. The death of Senzangakona prevented him from fulfilling this promise. Zwide now demanded that Shaka should fulfil the promise. Shaka was not a man to be forced. When Shaka's refusal became known to Zwide he decided to teach Shaka a lesson. There was more than one reason which brought about the war between Zwide and Shaka. The defeat of Zwide was not an easy task and Shaka was aware of it, whilst Zwide on the other hand greatly underrated Shaka. Shaka was not prepared for a war but Zwide forced his hand by attacking him. The opposing armies met on the Qokli Hill.

THE BATTLE OF QOKIL HILL

Shaka· who was always on the look out knew that his refusal to send the girls to Zwide meant war so he started to prepare for it. He collected all his cattle and mobilised the whole of his people and sent them to the southern part of his Kingdom. Shaka left part of his army to defend the children, women and the cattle and he took less than 4,000 soldiers to meet Zwide. His opponent had about thrice his number. In April 1818 Zwide invaded Shaka's country near the White Umfolozi river. Zwide's men had to cross this river which was being guarded by the Zulus. The main army of Shaka was concentrated on Qokli hill. At this place Shaka drew up his soldiers in a circle some five or six times deep. There was tactical reserve hidden on the top of the hill. Shaka a born general had collected enough food and water to feed his army at this place because there was no water around the hill. Water could be obtained only at a considerable distance. He also took care to destroy and to remove every food around the hill. Shaka decided to engage the enemy at this place because his army was smaller than his opponent and could not arrange his soldiers in the plain. Shaka relying on the quality and the iron discipline of his soldiers decided to arrange his soldiers in a circle for the enemy to surround it. He did this because he believed in his soldiers and thought that they would be able to get out of the difficulty. By forming his soldiers into a circle he avoided exposing his flanks. Shaka knew that after the first day's battle his enemies would be tormented with thirst. The battle was fought at the beginning of April which was hot. He also knew that when thirst set in the Ndwandwes would not be able to fight well. Shaka stayed on top of the hill and decided that whenever his opponent made a mistake he would strike at once with his reserve. Shaka never believed in a defensive war or action, unless it was a means of deceiving his enemy to make a wrong move so that he could strike him with all the power at his disposal. He knew that if thirst set in his opponents would brake off the engagement to go and drink some water either at Umkumbame river, or the Umfolozi river. He made plans which were to be put into action as soon as this happened.

The Commander-in-Chief of Zwide's army was Nomahlanjana. The commander of the Zulu regiment was Ngoboka who was assisted by two other famous commanders called Ndlela and Njikiza Ngcolosi.

When the Ndwandwes left their homeland to meet Shaka and reached the Umfolozi river they plunged into it and attempted to cross it. The Zulus who were waiting at the bank of the river massacred them in hundreds. At this time Shaka arrived with 500 of his best soldiers — the Fasimbas for a personal reconnaissance. Mdlaka who was now second in Command was left in charge of the main army on the hill. The Ndwandwes had calculated that if they could hold Ngoboka here they could cross at another part of the river and fall on his back but they soon discovered to their disappointment that all the other places were well guarded. Nomahlanjana the commander of the Ndwandwes realized at noon that it was futile to attempt crossing the river so he retired. Many Ndwandwes perished whereas only a few Zulus died. Shaka ordered Ngoboka to retire and join the main army as soon as he discovered that the river was dropping to a certain level. Shaka joined the main army and studied the reports and the dispositions of the Ndwandwes. As soon as he had finished studying his reports he ordered that the soldiers should be served with food and fresh water. After the meal all the senior officers and commanders including Mgobozi, Nzobo, Ngomane, Mdlaka and Shaka attended a council of war. Shaka after the council went to sleep with Mgobozi also sleeping next to him. Ngoboka returned to pin the main body and went to report to Shaka who was then awake and sitting at the top of the hill facing the Ndwandwes. The commander greeted Shaka with a low Bayete and Shaka replied by saying "My old friend." Ngoboka told him that the river had dropped and could now be crossed at different places and that the only places where it could not be crossed were the deep long pools. Before Ngoboka came to report to Shaka he had ordered Ngoboka to leave observation pickets all along the river to report on the movements of the enemy to him. Ngoboka told Shaka that reinforcements for Ndwandwes had arrived during the night. After the report Shaka told Ngoboka that he had a plan to decoy a part of Zwides army from the main fighting force. Shaka said that early in the morning the Ndwandwes would see one in every four of the Zulu cattle being driven over the Tonjaneni Heights. The cattle would be guarded by 200 Fasimbas and 500 Nkomendala reserves. When the enemy discovered that it had surrounded the Zulus and thinking that the Zulu cattle

31

were being sent south-wards away from them, the Ndwandwes would send a large part of their fighting force to get the cattle. By the time the soldiers caught up with the cattle they would be twice the distance from the Qokli hill.

He also said that the running fight which would ensue would also delay the Ndwandwes. Before the enemy could be back again with the cattle, the main battle would have gone one way or the other at the hill. Shaka said that in order to decieve the enemy still further he was going to hide part of his force at the other side of the hill with the reserve. This would make the Ndwandwes believe that there were only 1,500 men whereas there were actually over 3,500 men on the hill. The commander of the force in charge of the cattle was ordered by Shaka to employ many ways including disappearance and reappearance to decieve the enemy. By disappearance and reappearance he could make his number of 700 look like several thousands. This Shaka thought would give the enemy the impression that his army was divided into two.

The news came to Shaka that the Nwandwes were crossing the river two miles away at two different paces. Shaka who was at that time having breakfast with his whole army stood up and said "Splendid! The Ndwandwes will think that most of the Zulus have gone with the cattle.".With his commanders flanking him Shaka proceeded to address the quarter circle of his soldiers. He stood with his face facing the enemy. In his address he laid great emphasis on absolute obedience and discipline. He told them to maintain their ranks closed and to keep their ears open for the commands of their officers. Shaka said that in the final chase there should be no formation to out-distance by more than half a spear's throw — the formation on either side. Any person who went more than half a spear's throw ahead the others, would forfeit his life after the battle even if he had been a hero in the battle. He addressed the reserve in the same way and told them to remain where they were and keep still until they were called.

Nomahlanjana, the commander of the Ndwandwes sent four regiments, a third of his force after the cattle as Shaka had predicted. The remaining of his army, eight thousand strong, crossed the Umfolozi river and assembled in a semi-circle on the north-eastern base of Qokli hill. Shaka arranged his force so well that only a small part of each regiment could be seen. Only half of his total force of 3,600 on the Qokli hill could be seen. The Zulus were drawn up in five lines. Before

Ndwandwes came Shaka ordered the four rear lines to come very close to the main line. The scouts of the Ndwandwes reported to Nomahlanjana that the hill was not heavily defended. The scouts also could not identify the various regiments because Shaka had ordered them to sit on their shields close to each other. The Ndwandwes thought that they would go through the Zulus just as a knife goes through a butter. Nomahlanjana told his officers, "It will be like slaughtering a lot of cattle in a kraal." The commander of the Ndwandwes ordered his men to advance within two spears throw. As they advanced their circle became jammed and a confusion arose. Their commanders had difficulties in rearranging them again. They were only one hundred yards from the Zulus. Shaka's men were sitting at their places in absolute silence. After their enemies had called them toothless dog Zulus there was movement but Shaka ordered them to sit back. The order was repeated by the officers. The enemy asked the Zulus to send out their champion to meet them and Manyosi with the permission of Shaka stepped forward. A champion from the other side also stepped forward to meet Manyosi. After he had advanced a quarter of spear's throw he hurled his spear at Manyosi who caught it with his shield. The Ndwandwe advanced further and pretended as if he was going to throw his second spear. Manyosi ducked behind his shield and the Ndwandwe waited for his face to reappear. He narrowly missed Manyosi's face when it reappeared. Manyosi ran after him and stabbed him with his assagai. Manyosi after killing this man shouted at the Ndwandwes "Who comes next?" Another man stepped forward and he suffered the same fate. Manyosi returned to Shaka. The whole of the Ndwandwes now advanced to engage the Zulus. Shaka now ordered his army to give battle. The order was repeated by all the commanders. The whole army rose like one man. The five line formation now seperated. Mgobozi was not among the attacking force. He had been ordered to be with the reserve. He did not like the place asigned to him and complained. Shaka sent a message to Mgobozi to come and join him in the front of the battle to see the boys he Mgobozi had trained. Shaka asked him to stay by his side but not to engage in the fight until he had given him the word. He said to him that he was to watch the soldiers fighting and to see where improvements could be made.

The force on the hill was commanded by Nzobo, Ngoboka and Ngomane. Shaka inspected all the fronts periodically and a perfect liasion was kept between the commanders. The enemy now aware of Shaka's strength advanced cautiously. These people were jammed. Shaka saw his opportunity and at once ordered his first line to attack. The first line was closely supported by the second line. The Zulus shouting their battle cry Si-gi-di! descended on their enemies and slaughtered them like cattle. Shaka moved from one place to the other to watch the fighting on all sides. Zwide's men fought gallantly but they lacked the iron discipline of Shaka's men. After sometime both forces began to trick the other. Each fell back as if they were obeying orders. The enemy withdrew to the foot of the hill and Shaka ordered his two front lines to go behind so that the third line now became the front line. Shaka collected all the spears of the enemy and then attended to the wounded. As the Spartan law commands those who were beyond the point of recovery were killed. If a commander was badly wounded they asked for his consent if he was to be killed before doing so. Those who were wounded were treated by the U-dibi boys. Over one thousand Ndwandwes perished in this engagement. Shaka inspected his force and gave them encouraging words. Shortly after the inspection the Ndwandwes attacked again and made the same mistake of throwing their spears. When the two ranks of the enemy had finished throwing their spears Shaka ordered his two front lines to attack. The Zulus again slaugtered their enemies. When the fighting stopped it was discovered that at least three Ndwandwes had perished for every Zulu. During this engagement Shaka stood at a place where he could observe Nomahlajana the Commander-in-Chief of the Ndwandwes. He also from time to time went close behind the front line to observe how the battle was going on. Zwide's men withdrew and were addressed by their officers. They were to march this time right up to the Zulus without throwing their spears.

As Shaka had thought and planned the Ndwandwes were beginning to feel thirsty. The sun was beginning to shine. Shaka welcomed the delays on the part of the enemies. He had calculated that when the sun really set in most of the enemy soldiers would go in search of water. This he thought would reduce the enemy fighting men. Shaka who was a man not to miss an opportunity said that he was going to strike the enemy with his fresh troops as soon as part of the enemy went away. Before the 700 Zulu soldiers with the cattle went away Shaka had arranged for some signals to be given to indicate the movements of the Ndwandwes. A smoke column on the far left flank will indicate the advance, and were to be freed as soon as the enemy came abreast of the spot. When the smoke columns started to appear on the right it would indicate their return.

The Ndwandwes who had been regrouping attacked again and Shaka threw his fresh two front lines on the battle field and ordered them to crush the enemy. When the two front lines were attacking Shaka sent in his third line. Shaka was left only with one line of reserve. The strategic reserve on the other side of the hill was not touched and was still intact. After this encounter two of the five lines of the Zulus vanished but the tole on the other hand was heavier. Nomahlanjana ordered his soldiers that in the next attack, after a short fighting they were to turn back as if they were afraid until they reached the bottom of the hill and then turn back again on the Zulus. The Ndwandwes advanced to attack again and after a short fighting pretended to run as they had been ordered. Shaka who was a born general discovered that it was a trick and ordered that his men were not to pursue the enemy more than one spear's throw. The Zulus who were always obedient to orders did not obey Shaka and pursued the enemy and inflicted a heavy toll. Most of the platoon commanders also did not obey the orders and joined the soldiers in slaughtering the enemy. Shaka was very angry with his men even though they had inflicted a heavy blow on the Ndwandwes. At the time that his soldiers were pursuing the enemy a smoke appeared on the right flank of the enemy force which had been sent after the Zulu cattle. Shaka thought that if the battle did not end quickly the returned soldiers of the enemy would be able to take part. He decided that if he threw his reserve force into the battle too many of the enemies would escape and would not be caught in the encirclement which he had in mind. Whilst the Zulus who had disobeyed his order were slaughtering their enemies they still maintained their formation. When the Ndwandwes turned at the bottom of the hill the Zulus killed them all. The Zulus now realized their position and started to run back. Within a short time they had climbed the hill and formed themselves into two solid lines. Their enemies fell back. The sun as Shaka had calculated now reached its climax and the enemy soldiers began to complain about thirst.

Shaka now inspected his soldiers and denounced their disobedience. In each platoon he condemned one man to die as a warning to the others. These condemned men were given the privilege of dying like soldiers with full battle honours. Shaka said that even though they had fought very well nevertheless discipline had to be maintained. The victims were to be selected by their captains and added that the platoon commanders also contributed their quota. Those selected were not to be killed by the Zulus. Each one before the next battle was to go one spear's throw in front of his former platoon, and there remain and fight alone till he was killed by the enemy. Those who had been selected to die went forward, turned round to face the main Zulu army and with their spears raised gave the Royal salute Ba-ye-te; and then turned to face the enemy and stamped the ground with their right foot for the last time.

Zwide's men assembled again to give battle. Only about one third of his original number was left. The Ndwandwes now had about 2,500 fresh soldiers. Their commander made a mistake of thinking that there were only about 600 Zulus now left and decided to crush them once and for all. Shaka who was watching the movements of Nomahlanjana saw some soldiers from the southern circle joining Nomahlanjana. He also saw the smoke columns on the right coming nearer. The time had now come for a decisive battle. The enemy soldiers now advanced twenty soldiers abreast. They advanced until they reached the foot of the hill. Nomahlajana used the semi-circle formation against two lines of the Zulus. The number of the column advancing was 1,500. Shaka had 2,000 fresh reserves. He decided to meet the enemy column with 1,500 soldiers and to keep 500 soldiers on the hill to face the chest column. He decided not to disturb his two-line circle round the brow of the hill. Nomahlajana was surprised when he saw the Zulus coming out from all directions of the hill to meet his men. The Zulus led by the Fasimba and Izi-cwe regiments on the left and right of Shaka surrounded the enemy with their commander narrowly escaping encirclement. The auxiliaries led by Ngoboka followed the Fasimba and the U-Dlambedlu came behin Izi-Cwe regiment. The Zulus who had been condemned to death fought gallantly and killed many enemies before they were killed. Mgobozi was allowed by Shaka to take part in this battle and provided him with a special bodyguard selected from Ama-Wombe regiment. Shaka included Njikiza the great fighter to watch over Mgobozi and restrain him in his actions. Shaka told Mgobozi to see to it that Zwide's young fighters did not escape. Mgobozi having completed the encirclement of the

Ndwandwes felt himself free to take part in the battle. The Ndwandwes fought very well but they knew that they could never win. Many Zulus died in this battle. The other commander whom Shaka had ordered to watch Mgobozi saved him on many occasions from death. Ndela fought on the right of Mgobozi and also distinguished himself very well. Nomahlajana ordered his forces to move from the hill of surprise. He soon came into contact with Mgobozi who with his soldiers massacred Nomahlajana and his four brothers, Dayingabo, Mpepa, Nombengula, and Sixoloba. The Ndwandwes surged forward to revenge the death of their five princes and in this encounter Mgobozi fell. He was not dead but buried under some Ndwandwe soldiers. Mgobozi after the battle was found by Shaka to be alive. At the end of this battle the whole of Zwide's force of 1,500 was wiped off with 500 Zulus dead.

The Ndwandwes who had succeeded in capturing some of the Zulu cattle were now sweeping down the Tonjaneni Heights. Shaka now thought that it was time to go and hunt down the Ndwandwes who had gone in search of water and were now coming back. Orders went to 1,000 soldiers who had remained out of the original 1,500 who faced the Ndwandwes to go and hunt down those who had gone for the water. Shaka now withdrew his two remaining lines and formed them into a semi-circle to face the remaining Ndwandwes. He threw every soldier into this last battle except 200 of less seriously wounded soldiers who were to guard the hill. The Ndwandwe Commander was told of the tragedy in the north and he at once issued orders for his soldiers to join the Ndwandwes who were returning with the Zulu cattle. The Zulus went after them but when they saw the returning Ndwandwes Shaka ordered a slow fighting retreat. Shaka headed for his Bulawayo kraal where he had ordered the Belebele brigade to meet him after they had finished the mopping-up operation. It must be said that the Ndwandwes who went after the cattle fought many times with the Fasimba and lost many of their men. The Zulus also lost some men. The original number of 700 had gone down to 400 who continued to press the Ndwandwes in order to get their cattle back.

At Bulawayo Shaka decided to make a last stand. He had 1000 soldiers at his disposal. The remaining 400 Fasimbas he ordered to go to the rear of the enemy. He ordered the Fasimbas at the rear to employ guerilla tactics so that part of the enemy soldiers would be diverted. Shaka learnt through his intellegence system that the Belebele brigade was returning back to his aid after having completed hunting down the water party. The Ndwandwe commander was now pressing Shaka with 3,500 fresh soldiers. In this battle the Zulu regiment which did most of the fighting was the Jubingqwanga. Manyosi who had fought like a lion before distinguished himself very well. He made his last stand in front of the door of the Royal hut before he was wounded. Shaka who always kept calm in time of crisis was very cool. The battle which was to decide his future was now being fought. He selected some soldiers and raced from one point to the other where danger appeared most. The Belebele brigade appeared at the right flank of the enemy and suddenly the situation changed. The enemy tried to break off the battle as the Zulus were now closing in on them on every front. The west was taken by the "Shorn Head Rings" regiment; the Fasimba party led by Nkomendala took the south; and the Belebele brigade barred the north and were spreading rapidly to the east. The enemy soldiers who escaped the encirclement were less than 1,00. The Zulus completely destroyed all the enemy soldiers.

After this victory Shaka returned to Qokli hill to survey how the battle was fought there and the number of soldiers who perished for the Zululand. The Zulu army which he had created had fought one of its real battles in their history. In order to find out how many people had died Shaka had to inspect the regiments the following morning. Shaka whilst he was inspecting the battle ground at Qokli hill saw "The Watcher of the Ford" a nickame given to the general he had ordered to protect Mgobozi. This man was guarding the place where Mgobozi fell. Shaka ordered all the soldiers who had been ordered to guard the outposts to go to the hill and rest. They saluted him and retired to the top of the hill. Shaka was now joined by his staff. Ngomane, Ngoboka, Mdlaka were present but Ndela and Nzobo were not there because they had been ordered to go after the Zulu cattle which the enemy took. He discussed all war reports with his war council and decided to stay on the hill for sometime as there was still 2,500 Ndwandwes at large. The hill was a safe place to be and he was not short of food and water. Shaka and his generals were sad at the loss of Mgobozi. Ngoboka asked for a report on the death of Mgobozi. Shaka told Ngoboka that the general he had ordered to watch Mgobozi was still standing on the spot where the great fieldmarshal fell and that they should

38

go there and see the body of their great friend and get a report. When they reached the place the "Watcher" stood sharply to attention and Shaka asked him "Where is Mgobizi" and the 'Watcher' replied "he sleeps with Zwide's sons beneath this mound of corpses". Shaka then said "I entrusted his life to you" and the 'Watcher' replied "In the last extremity I cried out the 'Great Elephants' command. Hark! my Father" Shaka at once noticed that someone was snoring and asked the "Watcher" to remove the corpses. After the corpses had been removed they found Mgobozi still alive and bleeding with wounds. Shaka now called out Mgobozi! Mgobozi! Mgobozi! and at the third call a voice came out saying "Yebo, Baba" Shaka then asked him what he was doing there and Mgobozi replied that the hill collapsed on top of him. When the corpses had been removed from him he sat up and placed his assagai across his knees and robbed his eyes. He looked around and then said "Hau! It looks as if there has been some fighting here." Next morning the evacuation of the hill began and they went to Esi-Klebeni military camp. At this camp Shaka and his officers met the Zulus who had gone after the cattle. They brought most of the cattle back. Shaka at this place inspected the regiments and found out that he had lost 1,500 killed, and 500 seriously wounded. Shaka continued to inspect the regiments and as he noticed there were so many familiar faces missing tears began to stream down his face. The enemy lost 7,500 killed. Shaka whilst the battle was going on had 1,500 soldiers who were guarding the women, children and cattle on his southern border. Shaka having inspected the regiments thanked them for their effort.

It was after the battle of Qokli hill that Mzilikazi a great general joined Shaka's army. In later years Mzilikazi founded his own nation called Matabele. His father was the son-in-law of Zwide who was treacherously murdered by Zwide. Mzilikazi before the battle of Qokli hill was paying homage to Zwide. As soon as he appeared before him Shaka took an immediate liking to him. Shaka who was quick to recognize men's ability gave Mzilikazi a responsible post in the Zulu army. Mzilikazi brought his people with him and they and others soon were incorporated into the Zulu nation. Shaka's army began to increase. Mgobozi began to train Shaka's army for the final show down with the Ndwandwes. The army was drilled and subjected to many manoeuvres. Mgobozi told the soldiers "Do I want to see you eaten by vultures and hyaenas after the next battle, merely because you were too stupid or lazy to understand that what I am trying to teach you today will save you tomorrow?" Shaka and Mdlaka also subjected them to strenuous field training. Zwide was not all the time sleeping. He also was busy preparing his army for the final show down.

Zwide was greatly disturbed because he was unable to defeat Shaka and it became clear that he would know no peace until Shaka was defeated. Shaka on the other hand fearing that Zwide might attack and destroy him at anytime kept on watching. When his spies reported to him that his enemy was on the march he gave orders to his people to hide and he destroyed all their foodstuffs. Ndwandwe army could not find Shaka's people. Having searched and walked for a long time the Ndwandwe army decided to sit down and rest. Some of them did not get up again. As soon as the army had fallen asleep, Shaka's army stealthily came out of their hiding place and set upon the sleeping Ndwandwe army. Being too dark to differentiate between friend and enemy in that hand to hand battle which ensued, there was a break and the Zulus stole away again. The enemy did not find the hinding place of Shaka's army and so moved away.

Shaka's espoinage system was par excellent. He had a friend called Noluju in the court of Zwide. Noluju was very powerful at the court of Zwide. Through his intellegence department Shaka knew that the Ndwandwe armies never carried much food when they went out on a campaign, they depended almost entirely on the food of the enemy. Knowing fully well that no army could fight with empty stomachs, Shaka and Noluju agreed on a plan of luring the Ndwandwe armies until they were exhausted. When the plans had been perfected, Noluju went to Zwide who was not aware that Noluju was a traitor and urged Zwide to attack Shaka. Believing implicitly in the discretion of Noluju, Zwide ordered his men to march against Shaka. The Zulus retired according to plan carrying away some foodstuffs and destroying all food along the way. Decoys were employed to draw the Ndwandwe army 18,000 strong along, but were commanded to avoid an encounter. When Shaka's army reached the Uthukela River they crossed and waited for the Ndwandwes to cross too. Ndwandwe army did not do this. They turned and began to go back home. When Shaka saw this he ordered his men to cross and engage the enemy. Shaka said to his soldiers "U! Children of Zulu, your day has come. Up! and destroy them all!" The Zulu force numbered 7,000 in this battle and the Ndwandwes 18,000. The Ndwandwes ran short of supplies but they fought very well. The two armies fought for two days but on the second day it became quite clear where the victory was to go. As soon as this battle had started Shaka a born tactican despatched a regiment to go and destroy Zwide's town and kill or capture Zwide. The regiment was to pretend that it was Zwide's regiment by singing the Ndwandwe war song. Indeed the Ndwandwe women were deceived and they came out in glee to meet their all conquering sons and husbands, only to be greeted with spears. Zwide only escaped death by hiding. He escaped and went very far from his burnt village. Meanwhile the Ndwandwes on the Uthukela River had been beaten by Shaka and when the Ndwandwe army returned home they found their homes ruins and ashes, and their wives and children corpses.

Shaka thanked his warriors and said that there was no need to search for cowards as they had all fought very well. He addressed his soldiers and distributed cattle among them. Shaka in addressing the soldiers said something about the history of Nguni. He said to the soldiers "Those who are not here are eating earth that we might live. Are we to forget the sorrowing mothers who bore them, and let their younger brothers and sisters go in want, because they gave their lives for our Zululand? Have we not a saying that a grieving mother's heart is soothed by a stomach full of meat? Well then, let us give to the bereaved the reward which the departed warriors would have received had they lived, and let us give a double measure, with both hands, to take the taste of bitter aloes from the mouths of the sorrowing ones." The soldiers were all very glad for seeing their great King honouring the dead. They shouted Bayete. Shaka now proceeded to distribute the rewards. He personally attended to the distribution. Shaka selected the very best cattle for the nation. After this he selected the best for the ordinary soldiers first. Second came platoon commanders, then the captains and so on upwards. The high ranking officers received the poorest cattle but by far the greatest number. Shaka laughed and told the senior officers that he was going to select some best cattle from the national property and give to them. The ordinary soldiers worshipped him for being fair to them. The soldiers who had fought very well in the battle received additional cattle for merit.

THE TRIAL OF ZWIDE'S MOTHER

After the gifts had been distributed to the soldiers and their officers came the trial of Zwide's mother called Ntombazi. This woman was captured when the Zulu army entered the kraal of Zwide. Zwide and some of his sons managed to escape. When the appointed day came for the trial of Ntombazi Shaka entered the Palace of Zwide and sat in Zwide's seat of judgment and she was brought before him. Shaka ordered her to be silent but the woman replied sharply by saying that Shaka should give the judgment first and proceed with the mockery of the trial. Shaka replied by saying, "True, you are judged, but I wish to hear your side and see if you can advance a single mitigating circumstance which may influence me in passing a sentence different from the one I have in mind." Shaka the Great then went on to mention the names of thirty chiefs whose head she had placed in her house. The names of the chiefs did not include Dingiswayo, Mashobane, Donda who had also been killed by Zwide with the consent of this woman. Shaka now began to question her: "Why did you have all these chiefs killed after securing most of them through treachery?" Ntombazi replied defiantly, "To gain power as you are doing now." Shaka asked "To gain power is a good reason, but why did you resort to treachery, and so make the good name of the Nguni people stink? Our laws of hospitality have never sanctioned such an evil thing." Ntombazi replied, "Power goes to the head and recks not what means it employs, as you too will soon know." Shaka asked "Why did you cut off those heads and mount them in your hut. It is an abomination according to all true Nguni customs. Only those who practice witchcraft resort to that." Ntombazi replied "I did it to gain the power of all those chiefs. If a chief is above the ordinary laws applying to witchcraft how much more so am I, a Queen, above them? How, then can I be accused of witchcraft?" Shaka asked "Your answers are shrewd, but tell me of what avail was all this witchcraft of yours against my better trained and better led army? Had Zwide relied more on training and equipment especially in our first war, you and he would not now be where you are. Witchcraft may help the weak to have faith in themselves, but beyond that it is useless against a stronger opponent." Ntombazi replied "How, then did we secure the mighty Dingiswayo?" Shaka replied to the question "You are ill-advised to boast of that foul deed. The downfall of that great King was due to his kindly heart and misplaced trustfulness. Often did I warn him that his generosity to Zwide and yourself would not, and could not, beget gratitude, any more than he could expect that from a wounded hyaena which he had nursed back to strength. Why did you urge Zwide to kill him and return evil for good?" Ntombazi replied "To gain power to secure the Nguni paramountcy". Shaka asked "Did you also have to desecrate his body by removing the head?" Ntombazi replied "Yes to gain all the power which lived in him". Shaka asked, "And your sons' son-in-law Mashobane, and my other friend Donda whom you invited to a love dance and then treacherously killed and beheaded?" Ntombazi replied "Also for power, and more power, which their heads would give me". Shaka asked, "And where is your power now?" Ntombazi pointed to her head and her heart. Shaka asked "Those of you who pratcice witchcraft make use of hyaenas as your mediums. Is that true?" Ntombazi replied "Indeed it is". Shaka asked "And you have complete power over these beasts?" Ntombazi replied "With emphasis. Absolute power". Shaka then said "That is good. You may return to your hut — your centre of power — and gaze on the heads of your victims. Perhaps you may even meditate on the reward for treachery, when your thirty silent witnesses bear testimony against you. Lest you be lonely, I will provide you with a like-minded companion to help you to while away the time. No hurt will come to you through my warriors, who will merely constrain you to remain in your hut. Food and drink will be provided for you only, but your companion will have to fend for himself." Ntombazi asked anxiously "What then, is the nature of my punishment?" Shaka replied quietly "That, you will learn in due course". Ntombazi asked "Have you captured my son Zwide? Is he to be my companion?" Shaka replied "Nay, it is nearer relative than that. Go now and partake of a good meal which will be given to you whilst your hut is prepared for you and your companion". Ntombazi before she went said "I thank you, O Chief!" Shaka replied sternly "Thank me not before you know the end".

Shaka had in the meantime ordered a hyaena to be placed in the hut of Ntombazi. When Ntombazi stood in the door way she was seized with fear and heard a smell of an animal though she could not see it. When her eyes became accustomed to the darkness in the hut she saw two dimly glowing eyes looking at her. She became more afraid and asked the soldiers who had been ordered to guard the place what was in the hut.

They replied that they did not know. The soldiers now opened a part of the hut to let in some light. Ntombazi now saw a big hyaena waiting to give her power. Ntombazi screamed and screamed. The soldiers came and she asked them to let more light into the hut. The soldiers agreed and more light was allowed into the room. The only things in the room were thirty heads of the chiefs she had murdered and two pots containing water one for her and the other for her partner. A strong guard was placed around her hut towards nightfall. Ntombazi asked for fire but she was refused. Food and beer were offered to her. Ntombazi gave part of her food to the animal and ate the remaining portion with the soldiers watching. The beer she drank but thought that too much of it would make her weak that she would be unable to prevent the animal from eating her up. Ntombazi also thought that if she could prevent the hyaena from eating her up Shaka might set her free. She decided to fence the hyaena off by feeding it with the skulls of the lesser chiefs. After sometime Ntombazi heard some steps coming nearer to her. Her fear increased and she shouted at the animal to go away. At last Ntombazi decided to end the agony by throwing herself near the cage of the hyaena so that it would devour her. The hyaena whose stomach was filled with the skulls of the chiefs turned away. The hyaena did not disturb her during the night. At eleven a.m. the guards called Ntombazi and said that her food was ready. They gave her the best food she wanted and insisted that she finished eating the food in their presence or returned it for anything she wanted. In the evening the soldiers gave her some food and this time she did not eat too much. She passed another night of fear by throwing more skulls at the hyaena. Ntombazi shouted and stamped to scare the animal. When Shaka heard of her actions he said "Hau! the old witch has a liver. Almost am I minded to pass her spear; but if she wins what am I to do with her, for I have sentenced her to be constrained to her hut only, and sooner, or later the venomous old serpent would strike back at me". Mgobozi replied to Shaka's statement "Burn down the whole evil place now, and be done with it I like not this infliction of many deaths on one person, even though she deserves it". Shaka replied "Nay, that I cannot do whilst she lives, for then I would eat my words, which said that no harm would come to her from my warriors." In the evening the hyaena tore off and returned with the front half of one of Ntombazi's feet. Ntombazi asked the guards to supply her with some leaves and bandage to heal her wound but the guards replied that they had orders only to supply her with food and drink. The guards told her that her case would be referred to Shaka. They came back shortly afterwards to tell her that her request had been granted. Shaka sent her a spear also. She also asked for a fire to be set up outside the hut and the request was granted by Shaka. The old wicked Queen now asked the guards as to the mood of Shaka. The old woman had by now drank too much beer and became more talkative and told the guards "I am going to kill that monster, but if I don't at least I will know that mine will not be the only chief's bones in its stomach". During the night the animal tore off another flesh from her. She bandaged the wound and now decided to face the hyaena boldly. She crawled towards it. The hyaena now saw her. Ntombazi screamed and laughed at the animal. Ntombazi made an attempt to spear the hyaena but it evaded her and got the spear out of her hands. Ntombazi after this knew that the battle had been lost and decided to wait for death to come to her. In addressing the guards she said "This beast will now eat me up piece by piece — Tell the King I thank him for the spear, but I received it too late. Ask him to have this hut burnt down speedily, so that once more I will be able to laugh, as I see my last enemy perishing in the flames with me". The guards returned to Ntombazi to tell her that Shaka had granted her request. By this time Ntombazi was in the dying state. The hut began to catch the flames and the hyaena began to go around wondering what was happening. Before she died with the hyaena, Ntombazi knelt in the middle of the hut and called out "Dingiswayo" and she died. The guards reported to Shaka that she had died and Shaka commented "She was an evil woman, but she was brave and died like a Queen.

Immediately after the Zulus had defeated the Ndwandwes at the Umbhlatwze river Shaka sent the female regiments to go and collect all the grains the Zulus had hidden in the mountains before the war began. They also collected the grains of the Ndwandwes. Once they had finished collecting the grains the great march to Bulawayo to Celebrate the victory began. Mgobozi told Shaka that he was the greatest Elephant then living and there was nothing beyond his borders which could stand against him. Fieldmarshal Mdlaka who was always cautious spoke to Mgobozi not to forget that the Tembus were on the Buffalo river and that if they formed an alliance with the Cunus and the Ngwanes they might be able to give the Zulus all the fighting they wanted. Shaka agreed with fieldmarshal Mdlaka and said "Well spoken, Mdlaka! Although we will celebrate our victory in a manner and on a scale never attempted before, we must not relax our vigilance till every tribe from the Kahlamba mountains to the sea owes absolute allegiance to us, or is exterminated".

When all the grains and cattle had been collected Shaka disbanded all the regiments for two nights for the female and the men to enjoy themselves. Once the time was up all the regiments reassembled and Shaka ordered the triumphant march to Bulawayo which was about fifty miles from where they were. Early on the third day after they had started with the 60,000 cattle they had captured from the enemy they arrived at Shaka's capital — Bulawayo. In front of the procession was the Royal cattle divided into different groups according to their colour. The army headed by Shaka and his fieldmarshals followed the cattle. The female regiments followed Shaka. Women and children lined up for about two miles from the Royal house and shouted praises to the soldiers as they passed. The cadet regiment were in full swing on the parade ground. Shaka's mother with Pampata besides her was siting on the high mound where Shaka used to sit to watch parades. All the females of the Zulu Royal family were also there. As soon as Shaka and his soldiers reached the parade ground he went straight to where his mother Nandi was sitting and gave her a hearty personal greeting before he turned around to great the nation. He also gave Pampata a friendly look. Shaka after he had greeted the people then mounted the mound and sat down on his throne.

The regiments and the people were drawn up to receive Shaka's thanksgiving speech. Shaka rose up and gave a report of the war and asked the people to celebrate the victory in a manner and scale that had never been attempted in Zululand. He said that there was enough food, meat, and beer for the people to enjoy freely. Shelters were built within two miles ridus from the Royal house and the military camps of the Isi-Klebe and Belebele regiments were only three and five miles away. Shaka said that there were places for the people to sleep during the night. Food and drinks were divided equally and reserves were kept under guard at the Royal Capital and the military camps. The people were supplied with different kinds of meat. There was plenty of singing and dancing which Shaka himself took part. Mgobozi and all the field-marshals were also there. On the second day of the celebration Shaka proclaimed that all the veteran soldiers who had proved their worth were to be allowed to marry and that he was going to pay for each person the necessary number of catle needed for one to get marry. The people applauded his decision. The selected one thousand veteran soldiers were allowed to choose their wives from the senior girls of the Vutwamini maidens' regiment. The soldiers were released from active military service.

Shaka then arose and strode in front of the regiments and then addressed them that because they had all fought very well he was going to relax the stern military rule for three days and nights. The first regiment to be disbanded for the stated days and nights was to be the "Lzimpohlo" Bachelors. After the expiration of the time they were to resume duty and then it was to be the turn of the Belebele regiment to be disbanded for three days and nights. Shaka disbanded all the maiden regiments (10,000) for six days. He told the male and female regiments that they may go and have sexual intercourse with the man or female of their choice. He said to them that they should behave themselves. If a soldier deflowered any girl the guilty soldier was to pay two head of cattle to the girl's father as damages and in case of the girl becoming pregnant the soldier was to pay three cows, so that the child and the girl would be provided for. Shaka said that in case the soldier decided eventually to marry the girl these fines were not to be regarded as part of the dowry. The fines were to be regarded as punishment for a lack of restraint. He also told them that as soon as the concession he had given them ended the old stern military law would be enforced again and any soldier who broke it would be put to death. After this statement Shaka disbanded all the maiden regiments and the Bachelors Division. The soldiers shouted Bayete! and the Bachelors Division melted away with the maidens. After the expiration of the concession all the soldiers returned to their camps.

After the victory celebration Shaka decided to overcome the Tembus. The Zulus met their enemy and defeated the Tembus. Shaka had now defeated almost all the people around him and in keeping with his status as the King of Greater Zululand built himself a new capital. He called it Bulawayo — the Place of Killing. Between the end of 1820 to the middle of 1821 Shaka undertook no military campaigns but centered his attention on organizing his country. By the end of 1821 he had finished the unification and consolidation of his kingdom.

Shaka now decided to conquer Matiwane, the chief of the Mgwanes. He put at the disposal of fieldmarshal Mdlaka, son of Nadi of the Gazini people to restore order in Natal. Mdlaka with his force crossed the Tugela river. After killing Nzasane Mdlaka caught Macingwane in the fertile plain of Kwa Cekwane. Macingwane escaped to the forest of Ntsikeni; Mdlaka caught up with him there and massacred his troops. Having completed his mission Fieldmarshal Mdlaka collected all what he wanted from the enemy country and sent them under a strong guard to Zululand. He turned his attention northwards to deal with Matiwane. Having meted out justice to Matiwane he returned to Zululand with many women, children and cattle. The women were settled in the various parts of the country and given cattle to make a fresh start.

Shaka at the time he sent Mdlaka to go and restore order in Natal also gave Fieldmarshal Mzilikazi two regiments composed mainly of Kumalos and other clans to display the might of Shaka in the north. This was the first time he gave Mzilikazi his first independent command. Before Mzilikazi left Shaka invited him to have beer with him and whilst they were drinking Shaka said to him "Son of Mashobane, you are a man after my own mind and I will miss you when you are away, for always our talks have given me a sweet heart. You have proved yourself to be a capable general under my command, but the time has arrived when you must act on your own initiative, of which you have plenty. This is necessary in order that you may win your own renown, and by conquering the north become my right hand there, and a great chief whose glory will not lessen, but add to mine. Still, I shall miss you sorely, my son". Mzilikazi replied: "I thank you, my father, for your words, which sweeten my heart and put a stone into my stomach". (which means to give strength and courage). Shaka wanted him to create a new black empire in the middle of Africa so that the two empires by linking together would embrace the greater part of Africa. Shaka never lost sight of his dream of creating a strong black empire. From the speech above it was quite clear that he wanted Mzilikazi to establish a new empire there. He did not want him to come back. Through many talks they had Shaka knew that he could rely on Mzilikazi. This is the main reason why Shaka never took serious steps to check the subsequent action of Mzilikazi.

Before Mzilikazi departed for the north Shaka gave him a new wardress similar to his own. Shaka and Mzilikazi now went to the parade ground where the two regiments were waiting. Shaka urged the soldiers to protect Mzilikazi. He said "Be you his shield like this new one I now present to him with, and his spear like this bright and sharp weapon which goes with it". At the time Shaka gave a new war-dress to Mzilikazi he also gave him a plume of white ostrich feather to wear in his hat. Shaka's own was a single crane's feather. After Shaka had finished the speech he took the spear and the shield from Mbopa and handed them to Mzilikazi. The shield was a glossy white with a single black sport in the middle. Mzilikazi thanked him by saying "Bayete! Ndabezita!" Shaka then took an ivory-handled axe from Mbopa. Shaka now addressed the regiments "Behold! this axe. It is one of my most cherished possessions. I present it now to my Child, as a token of my love for him, and as an emblem of his authority". Mzilikazi again thanked him by saying "Bayete! Ndabezita! and the regiments shouted Bayete! The axe is now in the Bulawayo museum.

Mzilikazi first marched to his own people the Kumalos. He attended to his personal affairs and after a day continued on his northward march. The object of the mission was known to himself and his chief of staff only. He learnt this lesson very well from Shaka. He conquered many people and a large herd of cattle. Instead of sending all the cattle to Shaka he decided to keep the best part for himself. Shaka's intelligence office reported this to him and he sent messengers to Mzilikazi to ask him to hand over the cattle which Mzilikazi refused to do. Shaka sent out the Lzimpohlo Brigade to bring Mzilikazi to him unharmed. The Brigade reported back to Shaka without bringing Mzilikazi and Shaka did nothing about it. Public opinion in 1823 was high and the Council of State compelled Shaka to do something. Shaka sent out the Belebele regiment against him. The regiment could not do better than the Lzimpohlo regiment. At last Nzeni a Kumalo who had a grudge against Mzilikazi betrayed his stronghold to the Belebele regiment and they surprised Mzilikazi and his soldiers. Mzilikazi and 300 of his soldiers escaped. They were joined by many women and children the Belebele regiment had spared. With these people Mzilikazi went inside Africa and began to build a new empire on the lines of Shaka. Next to Shaka he became the greatest King in the southern and central Africa and built an empire whose size was bigger than that of Shaka. He employed Shaka's method of nation building. He built his capital and named it Bulawayo.

By 1824 Shaka was undisputed master of the whole of Natal. It was at this time that the first Europeans visited him. The party included Nathaniel Isaacs, Henry Fynn, F.G. Farewell and King. The Europeans were highly impressed with the country they saw and Fynn recorded in his diary "We were struck with astonishment at the order and discipline maintained in the country through which we travelled. The regimental kraals, especially the upper parts thereof, also the kraals of chiefs, showed that cleanliness was a prevailing custom and they practiced this not only inside their huts, but also outside, for there were considerable spaces where neither dirt nor ashes were to be seen". When the party entered Shaka's Kraal they could not believe what they saw. Fynn wrote "On entering the great cattle Kraal we found drawn up within it about 80,000 natives in their war attire... It was a most exciting scene, surprising to us, who could not have imagined that a nation termed "Savages" could be so disciplined and kept in order. "Regiments of girls, headed by officers of their own sex, then entered the centre of the arena to the number of 8,000-10,000 each holding a slight staff in her hand".

Shaka asked the whites for what reasons they had come to his country and after many questions the visitors were invited to come under a big fig tree. With an interpreter Shaka seated himself on his chair and after the visitors had sat down began the business of the day. There were no bodyguards at this interview. Shaka gave them beef to drink and inquired whether their journey to his country had been pleasant. Shaka then told his visitors how well his nation was governed and that any subject could leave his property anywhere without fear of it being stolen. He told them also that in his country no man could molest the wives or daughters of another man. Shaka told his visitors that his capital Bulawayo was magnificent, that he had many cattle and a well disciplined army at his command to repell any possible aggressor. Shaka inquired from the visitors the political situation in Europe and other parts of the world. He made inquires about King George whom he called his brother. He inquired about the size of King George's army, his country and the nature of his government, the size of his capital and the number of his wives and cattle. The visitors told him that King George had only one wife and Shaka said to the visitors "That accounts for his advanced age;

but he would have been wiser still to have none at all like myself"... When Shaka was told of the extent of British Empire, and that the French Empire had been broken down, Shaka said "Yes, I see now, there are only two great chiefs in all the earth. My brother King George — he is King of all the whites and I Shaka, I am King of all the Blacks". After this interview Shaka told his visitors that he had built a special Kraal where they were to live during their visit. The visitors were conducted to this place by some soldiers. When they arrived the found a banquet awaiting them, namely, a sheep, an ox, baskets of ground corn, honey, groundnuts, potatoes, and three gallons of the best beer. The visitors fired eight gun salute in honour of Shaka.

The following morning Shaka sent a messenger to tell the visitors that he wanted to see them. When they arrived the visitors found Shaka and his people assembled. Shaka there and then repeated in public the questions he had put to the visitors in private, for example: "He desired to know from us if ever we had seen such order in any other state... He assured us that he was the greatest King in existence; that his people were as numerous as the stars, and his cattle innumerable." Shaka had many conversations with his visitors. Fynn records that Shaka said that "The first forefathers of the Europeans had bestowed on us many gifts by giving us all the knowledge of arts and manufactures, yet they had kept from us the greatest of all gifts, such as a good black skin, for this does not necessitate the wearing of clothes to hide the white skin, which was not pleasant to the eye. He well knew that for a black skin we would give all we were worth in the way of our arts and manufactures. He then asked what use was made of the hides of cattle slaughtered in our country. When I told him they were made into shoes and other articles, which however, I could not explain so as to make him understand, he exclaimed that was another proof of the unkindness of our forefathers, for they had obliged us to make use of hides to protect our feet, but as such protection was unnecessary in their case their forefathers revealed to them that hides should be used for making more handsome and serviceable articles, namely shields. This changed the conversation to the superiority of their arms; these he endeavoured to show in various ways were more advantageous than our muskets. The shield, he argued, if dipped into water previous to our attack, would be sufficient to ward off the effect of a ball fired when they were at distance, and in the interval of reloading they would come to close quarters, when we, having no shield, would drop our guns and attempt to run, but, as we are unable to run as fast as his soldiers, we must all inevitably fall into their hands".

At the end of their visit the visitors returned to Port Natal. Fynn remained with Shaka for one month before joining his friends. One night as Shaka was dancing he was stabbed. He was stabbed with an assagai through the left arm and the blade passed through the ribs under the left breast. Fynn was called to treat him. Shaka's own African doctors also attended him. The African gave the King a vomit and washed the wounds with decoctions of cooling roots. He also examined the wound to find out if any poison had been used on the assagai. Fynn says "Shaka cried nearly the whole night, expecting that only fatal consequences would ensue. The crowd had now increased so much that the noise of their shrieks became unbearable, and their noise continued throughout the night. Morning showed a horrid sight in a clear light. I am satisfied I cannot describe the horrid scene in language powerful enough to enable the reader, who has never been similarly situated, to apprecite it aright. The immense crowds of people that arrived hour after hour from every direction began their shouting on coming in sight of the Kraal, running and exerting their utmost powers of voice as they entered it and joined those who had got there before them.

'We then understood that six men had been wounded by the Assassins who wounded Shaka. From the road they took, it was supposed that they had been sent by Zwide, King of the Ndwandwes, who was Shaka's only powerful enemy. Two regiments were accordingly sent off at once in search of the aggressors.

"At noon on that day (fifth day) the party sent out in search of the would-be murderers returned, bringing with them the dead bodies, of three men whom they had killed in the bush (Jungle). These were the supposed assassins. The bodies having been carried off, were laid on the ground in a roadway about a mile from the Kraal. Their right ears were then cut off and the two pursuing regiments sat down on either side of the road, while the whole of the people, men, women, who had assembled at the kraal, probably exceeding 30,000, passed up the road crying and yelling. Each one, on coming up to the bodies, struck them several blows with a stick, which was then left on the spot, so that nothing more of these was to be seen; only an immense pile of sticks remained, but the formal ceremony still went on. The whole body now collecting, and three men walking in advance with sticks on which were the ears of the dead and now shattered bodies, the procession moved to Shaka's kraal. The King now made his appearance. The national song was chanted. After this a fire was made in the centre of the cattle Kraal where the ears were burnt to ashes.

"There now being every appearance of Shaka's complete recovery, the chiefs and principal men of the nation brought cattle to the King as offerings of thanks-giving; and on the next day the principal women of the nation did the same. Shaka then offered sacrifices to the spirit of his deceased father".

When Shaka had completely recovered he sent a force to destroy his enemy. A force of 4,000 strong was dispatched with orders to hide in the bush until they were joined by another force of 3,000 men. Once the soldiers had assembled a speech was made by Mbikwana. He told the soldiers that it was necessary to revenge the enemy. The soldiers were ordered not to spare neither man, woman, child nor dog. They were told to wipe out the enemy towns' from the map. The command was given to an elderly chief called Benziwa. The force moved into the enemy's country.

Fynn says that "During Shaka's illness a carpenter in the employ of Mr. Farwell arrived at his residence. He had been sent to built for Shaka a house like those used by Europeans. He brought with him a saw, a hammer, a gimlet, and an adze, also some nails. Shaka wished to know the use of these things, except the hammer, for he knew that a tool of that description was used by Zulu blacksmiths. After the uses of the gimlet and nails had been explained, he sent for a piece of the hardest wood grown in his country, namely, a species of ironwood. He desired that the gimlet should be tried on that. It snapped at once. Then he said the nails must be used without the gimlet. These, on being hammered, bent into all kinds of shapes. Much pleased with his own cunning, he declined to have the house built, directing the carpenter to build them in England where the wood was softer than the iron and not attempt to build in Zululand where our iron was softer than his wood. After this, he frequently talked of sending six of his men to build a house for King George in the Zulu style, for, though assured that King George's houses were much larger than his, he would not be convinced that they were as neatly constructed."

After Shaka had completely recovered his European visitors left him and returned to Port Natal. Shaka summoned his council and discussed the visit of the White men. Later Ngoboka, fieldmarshal Mdlaka, Mgobozi and Shaka discussed the firearms and the use of horses in war. Shaka was thinking seriously of sending some of his soldiers to his brother King George to learn the use of fire arms. He at the same time suggested that the King should also send some of his men to Zululand so that he would train them in guerrilla warfare. He said that the white man's tanks were useful in an open warfare whilst they were useless in guerrilla warfare. He also thought seriously of opening schools in his Kingdom to learn all things. He was always prepared to learn new things. When Shaka had finished discussing matters with his generals he decided on a force route march throughout his kingdom. The whole of his council, his generals and 30,000 soldiers were to accompany him. He handed the affairs of the state to his famous field-marshal Mdlaka. Shaka and his company marched 300 miles within six days. He inspected all the military camps. As soon as he returned to Bulawayo he ordered fieldmarshal Mdlaka to take seven regiments to go to the aid of Mosheshe, the King of the Basutos who was being attacked by Matiwane. Mosheshe had asked Shaka for protection by saying that Shaka should "Throw his blanket over him". He acknowledged Shaka as his overlord. The place Shaka had ordered Mdlaka to go was five hundred miles from Zululand. Mdlaka after crossing the Drakensberg mountains engaged the enemy at Likhoele, not far from Lady-brand and again at Kolonyama. Mdlaka captured all the cattle of the Ngwanes. Mdlaka pursued Matiwane and after about six hundred miles away from his base he decided to return. On his way back to Zululand he paid a friendly visit to Mosheshe at Ntaba Bosiu and told him that Shaka would continue to protect him. Mosheshe began to rise by diplomatic means than by war, attaching his own people to him by the justice and mildness of his rule — and by the same means attracted first malcontents from other chiefs and later the whole people until from small beginning he built up the Basuto nation.

SIKHUNYANA SUCCEEDS ZWIDE

Zwide died without appointing his successor. The heir apparent had died at Qokli. Zwide left two sons called Sikhun-yana and Somaphunga. There was a dispute as to which one should succeed his father. It became quite clear to Somaphunga that his brother wanted to take his father's place. Somaphunga got to know that his life was in danger so he decided to put himself under the power of the man who had defeated his father — Shaka. Shaka received him kindly and gave him a cattle and a wife. Because of this, Shaka became known as Indlovu ethe imuka babeyilandela abakwaLanga (The elephant which as it went away those of Langa followed.)

Sikhunyana became king and feeling himself strong decided to meet Shaka on a battlefield. Sikhunyana went to Ezindolowane and Encake hills, and decided to wait. His aim was to draw Shaka to this place. Shaka went and made a halt at Nobamba where the army was briefed and then marched on to the battlefield. Sikhuyana was defeated and he fled to Tembeland with the Zulus following him. The Zulus overtook him but he deceived them and he went up north to Soshangana where he was later killed. Both Zwide and his son Sikhunyana never died in their own country.

In this battle Shaka had a force of 40,000 soldiers and his opponent had the same number. Shaka commanded the main division of his army with Ndlela and Nzobo each commanding a wing. Mdlaka commanded the second division. Mgobozi was at the side of Shaka. The Zulu army encamped at En-Tombe river within the vicinty of Ndolowane and Ncaka hills. The Ndwandwes assembled at the bottom of the hill. Early in the morning Shaka and his generals went down the hills to survey the position of the enemy. He discovered that his spies had reported correctly as to the enemy's strength. Sikhunyana had chosen a very strong position. Shaka with 20,000 soldiers faced the enemy whilst fieldmarshal Mdlaka with 20,000 soldiers in the north-west was encircling the enemy. Shaka returned to his soldiers in the afternoon from the place where he had surveyed the position of the enemy. He assembled his soldiers and told them of what he had seen and what he expected from them. Shaka asked for voluntiers who would clear a way through the solid phalanx of the massed enemy ranks. Fieldmarshal Mgobozi came out and after he had demonstrated how he would cut a hole in the enemy rank said "Thus shall I go, spearing my way through the serried ranks of the foe, until I emerge in their rear or die — and so must we all do for our Father." Shaka was worried for the safety of his old friend but as Mgobozi had voluntiered he could do nothing about it. Others joined Mgobozi. That evening Shaka, Ngoboka and

Mgobozi these three people who had formed a pact in their earlier days to protect each other sat together conversing. Shaka was very sad because he knew that Mgobozi would die the following day. Mgobozi said to Shaka "My father, we must all die sooner or later, and if my time has come nothing will hold it back. It is far, far, better to die with the joy of battle in the heart than to pine away with age, or like a sick ox in a kraal. I have lived by the spear and I shall die by it. That is a man's death. You would not deprive me of that, who are my friend as well as my father."

Shaka then said to Mgobozi "Go well, son of the Msane clan, who taught my regiments so well. You have been my dearest friend." Mgobozi wished his friends all the best and went to his quarters to sleep.

Early in the morning when the battle took place Mgobozi as he had promised to do with other volunteers bored straight into the enemy ranks. They inflicted a heavy casualties on the enemy. As the enemy soldiers turned against them Mgobozi and his people backed against a big rock and fought back. The enemy soldiers were ferious because they recognized Mgobozi as the man who had killed many of their princes at the battle of Qokli hill. Mgobozi fought like a lion. He knew that the safety of the boys depended upon him and after he had received some wounds urged them to fight harder. The main Zulu army was less than 100 yards away. When the main army heard the voice of Mgobozi they also fought like a lion to reach him before he was caught down by the enemy. By this time the enemy was falling one by one on either side of him. Mgobozi was now bleeding on many sides. When he looked around him there were only six of his men left. Mgobozi now said to his men "in the next clash we will all eat earth, For us the sun will rise no more, but I for one do not regret it. I have lived by the spear, and today I die by the spear. That is how it should be. Look at the 'mat' of corpses we have made for ourselves. It is a fit resting place for a King — and you are kings — all of you." Mashaya who was among the volunteers said to Mgobozi "My father, we all die gladly with you, for who would live when you are gone?" Mgobozi then addressed his men for the last time before they all died "I thank you, Mashaya; your words put a stone into my stomach, for I like not to drag you to certain death. And now, my children, let us say farwell, for the enemy is stirring and will soon be upon us. That will be our last fight. Let us call our final message to our brothers over there — a message of good cheer, for one more thrust will bring the Ndwandwe bull to his knees. Then let us give praise to our King. There after, my children, I will say no more, for I feel the battle madness coming over me, and already the whole world looks red to me, like the blood dripping from my body. Now, all together!" "U-ZULU! U-Qobolwayo! Bayete! Nkosi yama Kosi" (The Zulu! their very essense! Hail, King of Kings! Thy will be done).

When the main Zulu army heard this they knew that Mgobozi and his men were still there and fought very well to rescue them. Mgobozi went forward and kill many Ndwandwes. When he looked he discovered that all his men with the exception of Mashaya were dead. The two men fought the enemy and Mashaya was severly wounded and sank to the ground. Mgobozi was the only one left now. The Zulu army was drawing very near. Mgobozi with blood coming out from all sides still fought like a fieldmarshal and killed twenty enemy soldiers in the last clash before he died. Thus ended the life of Fieldmarshal Mgobozi Shaka's dearest friend and one of the best generals Africa has ever produced.

By the time Mgobozi died the Zulu army had reached the enemy and were stabbing them both left and right. The Ndwandwes were now running away and the Zulus pursued and stabbed them one by one. The Ndwandwes went on top of a hill and in front of their women and children made the last stand. They were massacred by the Zulus but Sikhunyana the chief and a few of his people escaped.

When Shaka heard of the death of Mgobozi he was very sad and went to look at the body of his dearest friend. His eyes were streaming and for a long time looked in silence. Shaka then said to Ngoboka that all the Ndwandwes who were then not yet dead should be killed. The Zulu army only talked of the glorious deeds of fieldmarshal Mgobozi. He was loyal and obedient to Shaka to the end. The Zulu army returned from the battle of Ndololwane in October 1826.

In November of 1826 Shaka built himself a new capital and called it Dukuza. The national First Fruits festival of 1826 was celebrated at Bulawayo because he had not finished building the new capital. The army was urging Shaka to finish off the remaining nations around Zululand. There were the Swazis, the Pedi-Sutus in the north and Faku whose territory borded that of King George's land. After the first Fruits festival Shaka send the army under field-marshal Mdlaka to the north to finish the people there. The aim of Shaka for sending the army, to the north was to demonstrate to the people over there of his power. Mdlaka after a short time withdrew westwards until they reached the Eliphants river. Mdlaka selected some of the soldiers leaving the rest there and went westwards and upwards into the middle highlands. As soon as Mdlaka left the Zulu army was confronted by Griquas led by Barend. Barends were then hunting elephants in the vicinity. These Griquas charged the Zulus with elephant guns. Because of the training of the Zulus and also because they had seen guns and horses before they did not run away. Fieldmarshal remembering the talks he had with Shaka decided not to fight the Griquas in the open field but withdrew his soldiers into the broken ground. Once the Griquas discovered that they could not fight the Zulus in the broken ground they withdrew and went away. This deprieved Mdlaka of putting Shaka's method into action.

The sickning force Mdlaka had left behind was surprised by the Sutus who killed many. The surviving ones joined Mdlaka's army which was now returning home. The army which had been away for three months reached Bulawayo and Mdlaka reported to Shaka on the 18th of March 1827.

THE DEATH OF NANDI

Nandi, the first woman to whom Zulu history assigns greatness died in October 1827. When the mother was struck with fatal illness Shaka was about sixty miles away. Messenger arrived to tell him that his mother was seriously ill. Shaka at once set out to go and see his mother. On the 10th of October 1827 before noon he reached Emkindini where his mother was already in a coma. Shaka ordered the regiments which had assembled around his mother's hut to their barracks and he sat with his elder chiefs in silence. He did not speak for two hours and after this period the news was brought to him that his mother Nandi was dead. Shaka with his eyes streaming retired to his hut alone and issued orders that the chiefs were to put on their war dresses. Shaka reappeared dressed in a simple war dress and his prime minister Ngomane announced to the nation that Nandi was no more. As soon as the announcement was made all the people present tore from their persons every ornament. Shaka now stood in front of Nandi's hut with his principal chiefs drawn in a semi-circle behind him. They were all in their war dresses. For twenty minutes Shaka stood there silently with his head bowed down upon his shield and tears ran from both eyes. He then broke into frantic yells and the chiefs and 1,500 people present began to weep for the female elephant. People came from all parts of the land to mourn and before noon the number of mourners had increased to 60,000. At noon the mourners formed into a circle, with Shaka in the centre and a war-song was sang. In the evening the body of Shaka's mother was laid to rest in a grave which had been dug near Um-Lahlankosi tree. Some 12,000 soldiers were present at the burial and this force was formed into a special regiment to guard the grave for one year. Nandi died on the 10th of October 1827.

When his soldiers returned from an expedition in the South-West, Shaka sent the army to the North-East. It was during this expedition that Shaka who remained at home was assassinated by his half brother Dingan and others. It happened on the 23rd of September 1828. Among the people who conspired to remove Shaka from the scene were Mhlangane and Mbopa. Some of Shaka's generals and counselors were killed on the same day. Shaka had built up the Zulu nation and the people liked him for that. They admired his great courage. But as the Zulus say: "Abantu abayi nganxanye bengemanzi" (People do not go one way like water). Some people were not altogether satisfied. Shaka who seemed to be always alive to the possible source of danger, in an inexplicable way over looked the most dangerous source, his own brothers.

Shaka the Great waged many wars. Once he had decided that there was to be only one King in the whole of Africa, he set out to translate his idea into reality. One by one he defeated the Kings. Within a short time his name became known everywhere. Shaka did not confine himself to Zululand but sent his soldiers as far as to Pondoland. Dingan did not wage many wars as Shaka. This may also be observed in his praises in which deeds of valour are not as numerous as in Shaka's. Shaka had done almost all the fighting at home and what little fighting there was left for Dingan was beyond the frontiers of Zululand.

Shaka dropped out of the picture just about the time that African affairs were becoming more complicated by the Great Trek. The war machine he had created, however, remained to play its conspicuous part for years to come. Within a space of twelve years he was able to conquer and unite an area larger than thrice Europe. His name became known everywhere. The mere mention of his name made people tremble with fear. Shaka the Great taught all the noblest disciplines of life... obedience to the law, order and self-restraint, submission to authority, respect for superiors, self sacrifice, constant duty and civil duty. In any Country, in any Age, Shaka would be a LEADER.

BIBLIOGRAPHY

SEE

HISTORY OF THE AFRICAN PEOPLE VOL. I BY
Professor G.K. OSEI

110621-300-6-60W